BEWICK'S
BRITISH BIRDS

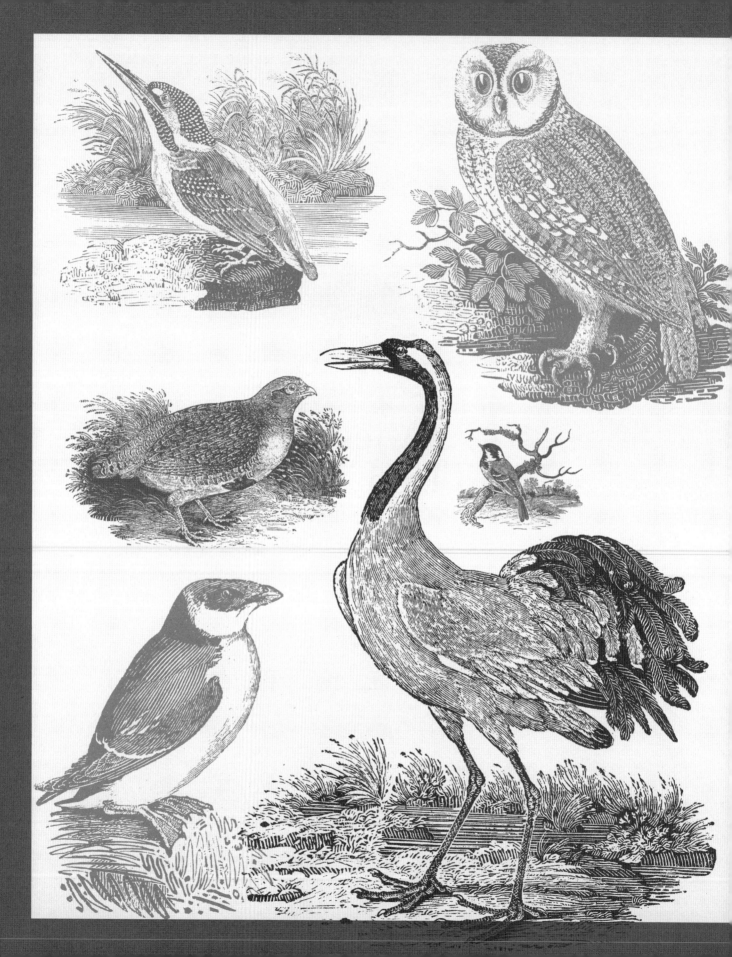

BEWICK'S
BRITISH BIRDS

THOMAS BEWICK

INTRODUCTION BY DIANA VOWLES

ARCTURUS

Diana Vowles is an editor and writer of 25 years' experience, specializing in art, gardening and natural history. She is the author of several books, including *The Country Living Handbook* (Arcturus Publishing) and two bestselling books that accompanied the Watercolour Challenge television series - *Watercolour Challenge* and *Painting with Watercolour Challenge* (Channel 4 Books). She is also a photographer, with a particular interest in studies of horses and the natural landscape. Diana lives in London and in Sussex, where she gardens, paints and photographs the seasons unfolding. You can visit her websites at www.dianavowles.co.uk and www.dianavowles.co.uk/writer

Many thanks to Dr Peter Friesen of Plattsburgh State University, New York, for the text of the 1826 editions of *Land Birds* and *Water Birds* used in this book.

All images are reproduced courtesy of Dover Publications, Inc.

ARCTURUS

This edition published in 2010 by Arcturus Publishing Limited
26/27 Bickels Yard, 151–153 Bermondsey Street,
London SE1 3HA

ISBN: 978-1-84837-647-2
AD001384EN

Printed in China

CONTENTS

LAND BIRDS

WATER BIRDS

INTRODUCTION

In the history of illustration, Thomas Bewick is a towering figure; nearly two hundred years after his death, there can be few people who have never seen one of his engravings used to accompany a newspaper or magazine feature, even if they are not familiar with the natural history books on which his fame rests. Collections of his work are held in museums and libraries worldwide – in Britain most especially in Newcastle upon Tyne, where he spent most of his life, and at the Cherryburn estate at Ovingham 12 miles away, now run by the National Trust – and his name lives on in two species of bird, Bewick's wren and Bewick's swan.

Bewick was born in 1753 at Cherryburn House, an eight-acre tenant farm and colliery beside the River Tyne. The eldest of John Bewick's eight children, he led the rural life typical of a boy in his circumstances, helping his father with jobs on the farm and in the colliery, and in his spare time exploring the wildlife and habitat with the keen eye and powers of minute observation that, once developed in childhood, were never to leave him.

While there was no training in art at his village school, the young Thomas nevertheless showed artistic flair, so at the age of 14 he embarked on a seven-year apprenticeship at Ralph Beilby's engraving business in Newcastle upon Tyne. There he learned all the skills that were necessary for an engraver, working with glass and various metals, but it was wood that proved to be the medium in which he excelled.

Woodcut printing had a long history. After the invention of the printing press by Johannes Gutenberg in 1440 it was used for book illustrations, but in its earlier form it was limited to the use of knives and chisels on a plank of wood cut along the grain. Ink was applied to the surface areas that had not been carved out and the wood was then pressed on to paper. The resulting image lacked the definition of printing by means of intaglio etching on copper, invented in Germany in the 1430s, where the finest lines could be drawn and ink wiped into them, to be transferred to paper under the enormous pressure of an etching press.

Although wood engraving was developed in the 16th century with the introduction of very hard boxwood carved across the grain, allowing metal-engraving tools to be used, it was only in Bewick's hands that it reached everything of which it was capable; he developed a technique of lowering areas of the wood block, giving variations of tone where the ink printed more lightly. Where wood engraving scored over intaglio etching was that the wood blocks could be cut to the same height as printing type, so illustrations could easily appear on the same page as text, and they were so hard that thousands of impressions could be made, something that did not apply to a copper plate. Given the enormous popularity that Bewick's books were to find, it is fortunate that the technique where his skills and interest lay was that best suited to multiple reproduction.

After the end of his apprenticeship and a brief and unhappy sojourn in London, Bewick became Beilby's partner in 1777, and following some early success with illustrated fables, he pursued his ambition to produce books on natural history. At first he mooted a picture book such as Thomas Boreman's *A Description of Above Three Hundred Animals*, which had found a wide audience at a time when there was much public interest in natural history. It seemed a dauntingly expensive undertaking for an engraving business, but encouraged by Solomon Hodgson, bookseller and editor of the *Newcastle Chronicle*, their project grew bigger; with Hodgson as a third partner to share the costs, they embarked on *A General History of Quadrupeds*, with 200 animals described in both text and illustrations. The book was first published in 1790, and by the time of the fourth edition in 1800 had grown to encompass a further 24 species.

In 1786 Bewick married a local girl called Isabella Elliot, a union that was to prove exceptionally happy and to produce four children. Emboldened by the success of *Quadrupeds*, which no doubt gave him confidence in his ability to provide for his growing family by means of his artistry, Bewick started work on his next huge project: a similar book on birds. In 1791 he spent two months at Wycliffe Hall, near Barnard Castle, where the late Marmaduke Tunstall had amassed a large collection of stuffed birds, many of them foreign species. However,

he found them badly stuffed and not suitable for reference material for life-like drawings. In his *Memoir*, published posthumously in 1862, he wrote, 'I had not been long thus engaged 'till I found the very great difference between preserved Specimens & those from nature, no regard having been paid at that time to place the former in their proper attitudes, nor to place the different series of the feathers, so as to fall properly upon each other. This has always given me a great deal of trouble to get at the markings of the dishevelled plumage & when done with every pains, I never felt satisfied with them. I was on this account driven to wait for Birds newly shot, or brought to me alive, and in the intervals employed my time in designing & engraving tail pieces or Vignettes.' Given this, Bewick and Beilby scaled down the project to include British birds only, produced in two volumes: *Land Birds* and *Water Birds*, with the overall title of *The History of British Birds*.

Bewick was fortunate to have friends in the Fourth Dragoons and a number of civilian sportsmen keen to help with the project by supplying the recently killed birds he wanted. The information in the text came from a variety of sources, notably the naturalists Thomas Pennant, Gilbert White and George-Louis Buffon, whose *Histoire Naturelle* was published in an English translation by W. H. Smellie in 1781. Bewick contributed his own observations, and Ralph Beilby also had a hand in the text; the latter's claim to authorship brought the partnership to an acrimonious end in 1798, a year after the first publication of *Land Birds*. Bewick took sole charge of the business, publishing *Water Birds* in 1804. A supplement followed in 1821.

Bewick continued to run his engraving business as a commercial concern, carrying out one more large-scale personal project – *The Fables of Aesop and Others*, published in 1818. In 1826, *Land Birds* and *Water Birds* appeared in their eighth and sixth editions respectively and after Bewick's death in 1828 at the age of 75 his

son Robert took over, publishing two further editions in 1832 and 1847. Thomas Bewick was one of those artists fortunate enough to be valued in their lifetime, and his family had taken good care to preserve not just his wood blocks but also his watercolours, pencil drawings and preparatory sketches – or at least some of them; he was wont to draw on his thumbnail, licking it clean to make the next sketch. This most skilled of engravers needed only the most basic planning before he picked up his wood block and tools.

Bewick's British Birds is a concise edition taken from the 1826 editions of *Land Birds* and *Water Birds*, the last to be published in Bewick's lifetime. Accustomed to wildlife books packed with high-definition colour photography, the modern reader will find a special delight in exploring the quieter subtleties of Bewick's work and the intensity of his observation of the natural world. While Bewick was a keen ornithologist who would take enormous pains to reproduce details of a species with unerring accuracy, he was also a countryman whose wisdom and humour could be allowed free rein in the charming vignettes that add so much to our understanding of rural life in the late 18th century.

Diana Vowles

TECHNICAL TERMS

An explanation of the technical terms used in this work:

To which are subjoined some of those used by Linnæus and other ornithologists, descriptive of the particular parts peculiar to some species

A—**Auriculars**,—feathers which cover the ears.

BB—The **bastard wing**, [*alula spuria*, Linn.] three or five quill-like feathers, placed at a small joint rising at the middle part of the wing.

CC—The **lesser coverts** of the wings, [*tectrices primæ*, Linn.] small feathers that lie in several rows on the bones of the wings. The **under coverts** are those that line the inside of the wings.

DD—The **greater coverts**, [*tectrices secundæ*, Linn.] the feathers that lie immediately over the quill feathers and the secondaries.

GG—The **primaries**, or **primary quills**, [*primores*, Linn.] the largest feathers of the wings: they rise from the first bone.

EE—The **secondaries**, or **secondary quills**,

[*secondariæ*, Linn.] those that rise from the second bone.

HH—The **tertials**. These also take their rise from the second bone, at the elbow joint, forming a continuation of the secondaries, and seem to do the same with the scapulars, which lie over them. These feathers are so long in some of the *Scolopax* and *Tringa* genera, that when the bird is flying they give it the appearance of having four wings.

SS—The **scapulars**, or **scapular feathers**, take their rise from the shoulders, and cover the sides of the back.

P—**Coverts of the tail**. [*uropygium*, Linn.] These feathers cover it on the upper side, at the base.

V—The **vent feathers**, [*crissum*, Linn.] those that lie from the vent, or *anus*, to the tail underneath.

11

Iris, (plural *irides*) the part which surrounds the pupil of the eye.

Mandibles,—the upper and under parts of the bill.

Compressed,—flatted at the sides vertically.

Depressed,—flatted horizontally.

Cuneated,—wedge-shaped.

HEAD OF THE MERLIN HAWK

1—The cere, [*cera*, Linn.] the naked skin which covers the base of the bill, as in the Hawk kind.

2—The orbits, [*orbita*, Linn.] the skin which surrounds the eye. It is generally bare, but particularly in the Parrot and the Heron.

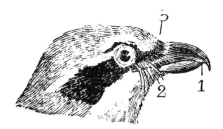

HEAD OF THE ASH-COLOURED SHRIKE

1—When the bill is notched near the tip, as in Shrikes, Thrushes, &c. it is called by Linnæus *rostrum emarginatum*.

2—Vibrissæ, (Linn.) are hairs that stand forward like feelers: in some birds they are slender, as in Flycatchers, &c. and point both upwards and downwards, from both the upper and under sides of the mouth.

3—Capistrum—a word used by Linnæus to express the short feathers on the forehead, just above the bill. In some birds these feathers fall forward over the

nostrils: they quite cover those of the Crow.

Rostrum cultratum, (Linn.) when the edges of the bill are very sharp, as in that of the Crow.

HEAD OF THE NIGHT-JAR

1—Vibrissæ pectinatæ, (Linn.) These hairs in this bird are very stiff, and spread out on each side like a comb, from the upper sides of the mouth only.

FOOT OF THE NIGHT-JAR

Showing the middle toe claw **serrated** like a saw. **Pectinated** signifies toothed like a comb.

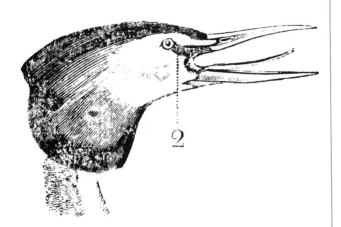

FOOT OF THE KINGFISHER

HEAD OF THE GREAT-CRESTED GREBE

Showing the peculiar structure, in the toes being joined together from their origin to the end joints.

2—The lore, [*Lorum*, Linn.] the space between the bill and the eye, which in this genus is bare, but in other birds is generally covered with feathers.

FOOT OF THE GREY PHALAROPE

Fin-footed and **scalloped**, [*pinnatus*, Linn.] as are also those of the Coots.

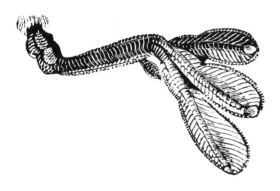

FOOT OF THE RED-NECKED GREBE

Toes furnished on their sides with broad plain membranes. [*Pes lobatus*, Linn.]

FOOT OF THE CORMORANT

Showing all the four toes connected by webs.

Semi-palmated, [*semi-palmatus*, Linn.] when the middle of the webs reach only about half the length of the toes.

Ciliated, [*lingua ciliata*, Linn.] when the tongue is edged with fine bristles, as in Ducks.

Nostrils linear,—when they are extended lengthwise in a line with the bill, as in Divers, &c.

Nostrils pervious,—when they are open, and may be seen through from side to side, as in Gulls, &c.

LAND BIRDS

THE GOLDEN EAGLE

(Falco Chrysaëtos, Linnæus—*Le Grand Aigle,* Buffon.*)*

This is the largest of the birds of prey; it measures from the point of the bill to the extremity of the tail, upwards of three feet; from tip to tip of the wings, above eight; weighs from sixteen to eighteen pounds. The male is smaller, and does not weigh more than twelve pounds. The bill is of a deep blue; cere yellow: eyes large, deep sunk, and covered by a brow projecting; the iris is of a fine bright yellow, and sparkles with uncommon lustre. The general colour is deep brown, mixed with tawny on the head and neck: quills chocolate, with white shafts; tail black spotted with ash: legs yellow, feathered down to the toes, which are very scaly; the claws are remarkably large; the middle one is two inches in length.

This noble bird is found in various parts of Europe; but abounds most in the warmer regions, seldom being met with farther north than the fifty-fifth degree of latitude. It is known to breed in the mountainous parts of Ireland: lays three, and sometimes four eggs, though it seldom happens that more than two are prolific. Pennant says there are instances, though rare, of their having bred in Snowdon Hills. Wallis, in his *Natural History of Northumberland* says, 'it formerly had its aerie on the highest and steepest part of Cheviot. In the beginning of January, 1735, a very large one was shot near Warkworth, which measured from point to point of its wings, eleven feet and a quarter.'

THE RING-TAILED EAGLE

(Falco Fulvus, Linn.—L'Aigle Commun, Buff.)

Is the Common Eagle of Buffon, and, according to that author, includes two varieties, the Brown and the Black Eagle; they are both the same brown colour, distinguished only by a deeper shade, and are nearly the same size: in both, the upper part of the head and neck is mixed with rust colour, and the base of the larger feathers marked with white; the bill is of a dark horn colour; cere bright yellow; iris hazel; between bill and eye is a naked dirty brown skin: legs feathered to the toes, which are yellow, claws black: the tail is distinguished by a white ring, which covers about two-thirds of its length; the remaining part is black.

The Ring-tailed Eagle is more numerous than the Golden Eagle, and prefers more northern climates. It is found in France, Germany, Switzerland, Great Britain, and in America as far north as Hudson's Bay.

THE WHITE-TAILED EAGLE

Great Erne, or Cinereous Eagle

(Falco Albicilla, Linn.—*Le Grand Pygargue*, Buff.*)*

Of this there appears to be three varieties, which differ chiefly in size:—the Great Erne, or Cinereous Eagle, (of Latham and Pennant); the Small Erne, or Lesser White-tailed Eagle; and the White-headed Erne, or Bald Eagle. The first two are distinguished only by their size, and the last by the whiteness of its head and neck.

The White-tailed Eagle is inferior in size to the Golden Eagle. The beak, cere, and eyes are of a pale yellow: the space between the beak and the eye is bluish, thinly covered with hair: the sides of the head and neck a pale ash, mixed with reddish brown: general colour of the plumage brown, darkest on the upper part of the head, neck, and back; quill feathers very dark; breast irregularly marked with white spots; tail white: the legs, which are of a bright yellow, are feathered a little below the knees; claws black.

This bird inhabits all the northern parts of Europe, and is found in Scotland and other parts of Great Britain. It is equal in strength and vigour to the Common Eagle, but more furious; and is said to drive its young ones from the nest, after having fed them only a very short time. It has commonly two or three young, and builds its nest upon lofty trees.

THE SEA EAGLE

(Falco Ossifragus, Linn.—*L'Ofraie,* Buff.*)*

This bird is nearly as large as the Golden Eagle, measuring in length three feet and a half, but its expanded wings do not reach above seven feet. The bill is large, much hooked, and bluish: irides in some light hazel, in others yellow: a row of strong bristly feathers hangs from its under mandible next to its throat, whence it has been termed the Bearded Eagle: the top of the head and back part of the neck are dark brown, inclining to black: the feathers on the back are variegated by a lighter brown, with dark edges; scapulars pale brown, the edges nearly white; breast and belly whitish, with irregular spots of brown; tail feathers dark brown, the outer edges of the exterior feathers whitish; quill feathers and thighs dusky; legs and feet yellow; the claws, which are large, and form a complete semicircle, are of a shining black.

It is found in various parts of Europe and America: is said to lay only two eggs during the whole year, and frequently produces only one bird; it is however widely dispersed, and was met with at Botany Island by Captain Cook. It lives chiefly on fish: its usual haunts are by the seashore; it also frequents the borders of large lakes and rivers; and is said to see so distinctly in the dark, as to be able to pursue and catch its prey during the night. The story of the Eagle, brought to the ground after a severe conflict with a cat, which it had seized and taken up into the air with its talons, is very remarkable. Mr Barlow, who was an eyewitness of the fact, made a drawing of it, which he afterwards engraved.

THE OSPREY

Bald Buzzard, Sea Eagle, or Fishing Hawk

(Falco Haliaëtus, Linn.—*Le Balbuzzard,* Buff.*)*

The length of the male is twenty-two inches, the female about two feet; breadth above five: bill black, cere blue, eye yellow: crown of the head white, marked with oblong dusky spots; the cheeks, and all the under parts of the body, are white, slightly spotted with brown on the breast; from the corner of each eye a streak of dark brown extends down the sides of the neck towards the wing; the upper part of the body is brown; the two middle tail feathers the same; the others are marked on the inner webs with alternate bars of brown and white: legs very short and thick, being only two inches and a quarter long, and two inches in circumference; they are of a pale blue; claws black: outer toe larger than the inner one, and turns easily backward, by which means this bird can more readily secure its slippery prey.

Buffon observes that the Osprey is the most numerous of the large birds of prey, and is scattered over Europe, from Sweden to Greece, and that it is found even in Egypt and Nigritia. Its haunts are on the seashore, and on the borders of rivers and lakes: its principal food is fish; it darts upon its prey with great rapidity, and undeviating aim. The Italians compare its descent upon the water to a piece of lead falling upon that element, and distinguish it by the name of Aquila Piumbina, or the Leaden Eagle. It builds its nest on the ground, among reeds, and lays three or four eggs, of an elliptical form, rather less than those of a hen. The Carolina and Cayenne Ospreys are varieties of this species.

THE PEREGRINE FALCON

Passenger Falcon

(Falco peregrinus, Linn.—*Le Faucon pelerin,* Buff.*)*

This bird has greatly the look of the Hobby Hawk, but is larger: length eighteen inches, breadth three feet six and a half inches, weight two and a quarter pounds. The bill is pale blue, tipped black; it is short, strong, and much notched. The irides are dark; orbits and cere yellow: the head, hinder part of the neck and cheeks are brownish black, with a stripe of that colour falling down from the cheeks and corners of the mouth, before the auriculars, each side of the throat. The upper plumage is dingy bluish ash, more or less clouded and barred with dark brown, and the shaft of each feather black. The bastard wing and primary and secondary quills appear at first to be uniform plain dark ash-coloured brown, but on a nearer inspection, the whole are seen to be barred with darker spots, and tipped dull white. The rump and tail coverts are more distinctly barred, and of a lighter colour than the other upper parts. The tail, which has twelve feathers, is a dark dingy ash, barred or spotted with brownish black, and tipped with pale brown or dirty white. The under parts of the plumage are pale clay colour, plain on the auriculars, chin, and fore part of the neck; towards the breast, the feathers are slightly marked with small scratches of black, and the breast with roundish black spots. The sides, belly, and insides of the wings are dull white, barred with dark brown; the primary and secondary quills, on the inside, are also barred, with ash and dingy freckled white. The thighs are long, marked with small heart-shaped spots; legs and toes short, strong and yellow; claws black.

THE BUZZARD

Puttock

(Falco Buteo, Linn.—*La Buse,* Buff.*)*

Buffon distinguishes the Kites and the Buzzards from the Eagles and Hawks by their habits and dispositions, which he compares to those of the Vultures. Though possessed of strength, agility, and weapons to defend themselves, they are cowardly and inactive; they will fly before a Sparrowhawk, and when overtaken, will suffer themselves to be beaten, and even brought to the ground, without resistance.

The Buzzard is about twenty inches in length, breadth four feet and a half. Its bill is of a lead grey; eyes pale yellow: upper parts of the body dusky brown; wings and tail marked with bars of a darker hue; the under parts pale, variegated with light reddish brown: legs yellow; claws black. But birds of this species are subject to great variations, as scarcely two are alike: some are entirely white; of others the head only is white; and others again are mottled with brown and white.

This well-known bird is of a sedentary disposition: it continues many hours perched upon a tree or eminence, whence it darts upon the game that comes within its reach: it feeds on birds, small quadrupeds, reptiles, and insects. Its nest is constructed with small branches, lined with wool and other soft materials; it lays two or three eggs, whitish, spotted with yellow. It feeds and tends its young with great assiduity.

The editor was favoured with one of these birds by John Trevelyan, Esq. of Wallington, by whom it was shot in the act of devouring its prey – a Partridge it had just killed.

THE MOOR BUZZARD

Duck hawk, or White-headed Harpy

(Falco æruginosus, Linn.—*Le Busard*, Buff.)

Length about twenty-two inches, breadth of the female four feet five and a half inches. The bill black; cere and eyes yellow; crown of the head yellowish white, lightly tinged with brown; throat of a light rust colour; the rest of the plumage reddish brown, with pale edges; greater wing coverts tipped with white: legs yellow; claws black.

Birds of this kind vary much: in some, the crown and back part of the head are yellow; and in one described by Latham, the whole bird was uniformly of a chocolate brown, with a tinge of rust colour. The above figure and description were taken from a very fine living bird, sent for the use of this work by the late John Silvertop, Esq. of Minster-Acres, Northumberland.

The Moor Buzzard preys on rabbits, on young wild ducks, and other water fowl; and likewise feeds on fish, frogs, reptiles, and even insects: its haunts are in hedges and bushes near pools, marshes, and rivers that abound with fish. It builds its nest a little above the surface of the ground, or in hillocks covered with thick herbage: and lays three or four eggs of a whitish colour, irregularly sprinkled with dusky spots. Though smaller, it is bolder and more active than the Common Buzzard, and, when pursued, faces its antagonist, and makes a vigorous defence.

THE GOSHAWK

(Falco palumbarius, Linn.—*L'Autour*, Buff.)*

Length of the female from one foot ten inches to two feet, the male is a third less: the bill blue, tipped with black; cere green; eyes yellow; a whitish line passes over each eye: the head and all the upper parts are of a deep brown; each side of the neck is irregularly marked with white: the breast and belly are white, with a number of wavy lines or bars of black; the tail long, of an ash colour, and crossed with four or five dusky bars; legs yellow, claws black; the wings are much shorter than the tail. Buffon, who brought up two young birds of this kind, makes the observation: 'The Goshawk, before it has shed its feathers, that is in its first year, is marked on the breast and belly with longitudinal brown spots; but after it has had two moultings they disappear, and their place is occupied by transverse bars, which continue during the rest of its life.' He observes further, 'though the male was much smaller than the female, it was fiercer and more vicious. Feeds on mice and small birds, and eagerly devours raw flesh; it plucks the birds very neatly, and tears them into pieces before it eats them.'

The Goshawk is found in France and Germany; sometimes in England, but is more frequent in Scotland; is common in North America, Russia, and Siberia: in Chinese Tartary there is a variety which is mottled with brown and yellow. In former times the custom of carrying a Hawk on the hand was confined to men of high distinction; so that it was a saying among the Welsh, 'you may know a gentleman by his Hawk, horse, and greyhound.'

THE KITE

Fork-tailed Kyte, or Glead

(Falco Milvus, Linn.—*Le Milan Royal,* Buff.*)*

Is easily distinguished from the Buzzard, and indeed from all the rest of the tribe, by its forked tail. Its length is about two feet: bill horn colour, furnished with bristles at the base; eyes and cere yellow; the feathers on the head and neck are long and narrow, of a hoary colour, streaked with brown down the middle of each; those on the body are reddish brown, the margin of each feather pale; quills dark brown, legs yellow, claws black. It is common in England, where it continues the whole year. Is found in various parts of Europe, in very northern latitudes, whence it retires towards Egypt before winter, in great numbers: it is said to breed there, and return in April to Europe, where it breeds a second time, contrary to the nature of rapacious birds in general. It lays two or three eggs of a roundish form, and whitish colour, spotted with pale yellow. Though the Kite weighs somewhat less than three pounds, the extent of its wings is more than five feet; its flight is rapid, and it soars very high in the air, frequently beyond the reach of sight; yet from this distance descends upon its prey with irresistible force: its attacks are confined to small quadrupeds and birds; it is particularly fond of young chickens, but the fury of their mother is generally sufficient to drive away the robber.

THE HEN HARRIER

Dove-coloured Falcon, or Blue Hawk

(Falco cyaneus, Linn.—*L'Oiseau St Martin,* Buff.*)*

Length eighteen inches; breadth somewhat more than three feet. The bill is black, and covered at the base with long bristly feathers; cere, irides, and edges of the eyelids yellow: the upper parts bluish grey, mixed with light tinges of rusty: the breast and under coverts of the wings white, the former marked with rusty-coloured streaks, the latter with bars of the same; the greater quills are black, the secondaries and lesser quills ash grey; on the latter, in some birds, a spot of black in the middle of each feather forms a bar across the wing; the two middle feathers of the tail are grey, the next three are marked on their inner webs with dusky bars, the two outermost marked with alternate bars of white and rust colour: the legs are long, slender, and yellow. These birds vary much; of several with which this work has been favoured by John Silvertop, Esq. some were perfectly white on the under parts, and of a larger size than common: probably the difference arises from the age of the bird.

The Hen Harrier feeds on birds, and reptiles; it breeds annually on Cheviot, and on the shady precipices under the Roman wall by Craglake: it flies low, skimming along the surface of the ground in search of prey; makes its nest on the ground, and lays four eggs of a reddish colour, with a few white spots.

THE KESTREL

Stonegall, Stannel Hawk, or Windhover

(Falco Tinnunculus, Linn.*—La Cresserelle*, Buff.*)*

The male differs so much from the female, that we have given a figure of it from one we had in our possession, probably an old one. Length fourteen inches; breadth two feet three inches; bill blue; cere and eyelids yellow; eyes black; forehead dull yellow; top of the head, back part of the neck, and sides, as far as the points of the wings, lead colour, faintly streaked with black; the cheeks are paler; from the corner of the mouth on each side a darkish streak points downwards; back and coverts of the wings bright cinnamon brown, spotted with black, much more so in some specimens than others; quill feathers dusky, with light edges; inside of the wings white, beautifully spotted with brown on the under coverts, and barred on all the quills with pale ash; the under part of the body is pale rust colour, streaked and spotted with black; thighs plain; rump and upper coverts lead blue, and the tail feathers

fine blue grey, with black shafts; towards the end is a broad black bar both on the upper part and under sides; the tips are white: legs yellow, claws black.

The Kestrel is widely diffused throughout Europe, and is found in the more temperate parts of North America: it is a handsome bird with an acute sight, and easy graceful flight: it breeds in the hollows of trees, and in the holes of rocks, towers, and ruined buildings; lays four or five pale reddish eggs: feeds on small birds, field mice, and reptiles: after securing its prey, it plucks the feathers very dexterously from birds, but swallows mice entire, and discharges the hair, in the form of round balls, by its mouth. This bird is frequently seen hovering in the air, and fanning with its wings, by a gentle motion, or wheeling slowly round, watching for prey, on which it shoots like an arrow. It was formerly used in Great Britain for catching small birds and young Partridges.

THE FEMALE KESTREL

This bird is distinguished from every other Hawk by its variegated plumage: the bill is blue; cere and feet yellow; eyes dark, surrounded with a yellow skin; head rust-coloured, streaked with black; there is a light spot behind each eye; the back and wing coverts are rusty brown, and elegantly marked with numerous undulated bars of black; breast, belly, and thighs pale reddish buff, with dusky streaks pointing downwards; vent plain; the tail is marked by a pretty broad dark ash-coloured bar near the end; a number of smaller ones, the same colour, occupy the remaining part; the tip is pale.

THE HOBBY

(Falco Subbuteo, Linn.—*Le Hobereau*, Buff.)

The length of the male is twelve inches; breadth about two feet; the tips of the wings reach beyond the extremity of the tail. The bill is blue; cere and orbits of the eyes yellow; irides orange; a light-coloured streak passes over each eye; the top of the head, and back, are bluish black; wing coverts the same, but in some edged with rust colour; the hinder part of the neck is marked with two pale yellow spots; a black mark from behind each eye, pointing forward, is extended down on the neck; the breast and belly are pale, marked with dusky streaks; the thighs rusty, with long dusky streaks; wings brown; the two middle tail feathers deep dove colour, the others barred with rusty, and tipped with white; the legs and feet are yellow. The female is much larger, and the spots on her breast more conspicuous than those of the male.

The Hobby breeds with us, lays three or four bluish white eggs, irregularly spotted with grey and olive, and is said to emigrate in October. It was formerly used in falconry, chiefly for Larks and other small birds, which were caught in a singular manner: when the Hawk was cast off, the Larks, fixed to the ground through fear, became an easy prey to the fowler, who drew a net over them. Buffon says, that it was used in taking Partridges and Quails.

THE SPARROWHAWK

(Falco Nisus, Linn.—L'Epervier, Buff.)

Length of the male twelve inches; the female fifteen. The bill is blue, furnished with bristles at the base, which overhang the nostrils; eyes bright orange; head flat at the top, and above each eye is a strong bony projection, as if intended to secure it from external injury: from this projection a few scattered spots of white form a faint line running backward towards the neck: the top of the head and all the upper parts are of a dusky brown; on the back part of the head there is a faint line of white; the scapulars are marked with two spots of white on each feather; the greater quill feathers and tail are dusky, with four bars of a darker hue on each; the inner webs of all the quills are marked with two or more large white spots; the tips of the tail feathers white; the breast, belly, and under coverts of the wings and thighs are white, beautifully barred with brown; the throat is faintly streaked with brown: legs and feet yellow; claws black.

The above description is of a female: the male differs in size: the upper part of his body is of a dark lead colour, and the bars on his breast are more numerous.

The female builds her nest in hollow trees, high rocks or lofty ruins, sometimes in the old nest of a crow, and generally lays four or five eggs spotted with red at the thicker end.

The Sparrowhawk is numerous in various countries, from Russia to the Cape of Good Hope. It is bold and spirited, but can be easily trained to hunt Partridges and Quails; it makes great destruction among Pigeons, young poultry, and small birds of all kinds.

THE MERLIN

(Falco Æsalon, Linn.—*L'Emérillon*, Buff.)

The Merlin is the smallest of the Hawk kind in this country, scarcely exceeding the size of a Blackbird. The bill is blue; cere and irides yellow: head rust-colour, streaked with black; back and wings of a deepish brown, tinged with ash, streaked down the shafts with black, and edged with rusty: quill feathers dark, tipped and margined on the inner webs with reddish white; breast and belly yellowish white, with ferruginous streaks pointing downwards; the tail is long, and marked with alternate dusky and pale bars; the wings when closed, do not reach quite to the end of the tail: legs yellow; claws black.

The Merlin, though small, is not inferior in courage to any of the Falcon tribe. It was used for taking Larks, Partridges, and Quails, which it would frequently kill by one blow, striking them on the breast, head, or neck. Buffon observes that this bird differs from the Falcons, and all the rapacious kind, in the male and female being of the same size. The Merlin does not breed here, but visits us in October; it flies low, and with great celerity and ease. It preys on small birds; breeds in woods, and lays five or six whitish eggs, marbled at the end with greenish brown.

THE EAGLE OWL
Great-eared Owl
(Strix Bubo, Linn.—*Le Duc, ou Grand Duc*, Buff.*)*

I s one of the largest of the British Owls, and has a powerful as well as a dignified look. The tufts or ear feathers are more than two inches long. The bill is strong, much hooked, and black; claws the same; irides reddish yellow; legs very stout, and covered with a great thickness of short mottled brown feathers; toes the same down to the claws. The predominant colours of the plumage are very dark brown and ferruginous, but mixed and beautifully variegated with markings and shades of black, brown, and yellow, with spots of white, crossed with zig-zag lines, and innumerable minute specklings of white, ash-grey, and brown. The outline of our figure was taken from a living bird exhibited in a show, the markings of the plumage from a very ill-stuffed specimen, which was taken on the coast of Norway, and obligingly lent to this work by Captain Wm Gilchrist, of this port. This bird is sometimes met with in the Northern Scottish isles, where it preys upon Rabbits and Grouse, which are numerous there, but it is very rarely seen in England: it generally lays two or three eggs; Temminck says they are white.

THE LONG-EARED OWL

(Strix Otus, Linn.—*Le Hibou,* Buff.*)*

Length fourteen inches; breadth about three feet. The bill is black; irides bright yellow; the radiated circle round each eye is of a light cream colour, in some parts tinged with red; between the bill and the eye there is a circular streak of dark brown; another circle of dark rusty brown entirely surrounds the face; its ear tufts consist of six feathers, closely laid together, of a dark brown, tipped and edged with yellow; the upper part of the body is beautifully pencilled with fine streaks of white, rusty, and brown; the breast and neck are yellow, finely marked with dusky streaks, pointing downwards; the belly, thighs, and vent feathers of a light cream colour: there are four or five large white spots upon each wing; the quill and tail feathers are marked with dusky and reddish bars: the legs are feathered down to the claws, which are very sharp; the outer claw is moveable, and may be turned backwards.

This bird is common in various parts of Europe, as well as in this country; its usual haunts are in old ruined buildings, in rocks, and in hollow trees. Buffon observes, that it seldom constructs a nest of its own, but not unfrequently occupies that of the Magpie: it lays four or five white eggs, rounded at the ends; the young are at first white, but acquire their natural colour in about fifteen days.

THE SHORT-EARED OWL

(Strix brachyotos, Gm. Linn.*)*

Length fourteen inches; breadth three feet. The head is small, and Hawk-like; bill dusky; the irides are bright yellow, and when the pupil is contracted, shine like gold: the circle round each eye is dirty white, with dark streaks pointing outwards; round the eye is a circle of black; the ear tufts consist of not more than three feathers, pale brown or tawny, with a dark streak in the middle; the upper part of the body is variously marked with dark brown and tawny, the feathers mostly edged with the latter; the breast and belly are pale yellow, marked with dark longitudinal streaks, most numerous on the breast: the legs and feet are covered with pale yellow feathers; claws much hooked, and black: the wings are long, and extend beyond the tail; quills marked with alternate bars of dusky and pale brown; the tail is likewise marked, and the middle feathers are distinguished by a dark spot in the centre of the yellow space; the tip white. In several specimens, both sexes had upright ear tufts: in one which was alive, they appeared more erect while the bird was undisturbed; but when frightened, were scarcely to be seen: in dead birds they were hardly discernible.

This rare and beautiful species visits us only in the latter part of the year, and disappears in spring. It has been known to breed in Northumberland, the young having been taken before they were able to fly. It flies by day, and sometimes is seen in flocks: twenty-eight were once counted in a turnip-field in November. It is found chiefly in mountainous or wooded countries: its food is principally field mice.

THE YELLOW OWL

Barn Owl, White Owl, Gillihowlet, Church, or Screech Owl

(Strix flammea, Linn.—*L'Effraie, ou Fresaie,* Buff.)

Length fourteen inches. Bill pale horn colour; eyes dark; the radiated circle round the eye is composed of feathers of the most delicate softness, and perfectly white; the head, back, and wings are yellow buff, beautifully powdered with very fine grey and brown spots, intermixed with white; the breast, belly, and thighs are white; on the former are a few dark spots; the legs are feathered down to the toes, which are covered with short hairs; the wings extend beyond the tail, which is short, and marked with alternate bars of dusky and white; the claws are white. Birds of this kind vary considerably: of several which we examined, the differences were very conspicuous, the colours being more or less faint according to the age of the bird; the breast in some was white, without spots – in others pale yellow.

The Yellow Owl is often seen in the most populous towns, frequenting churches, old houses, maltings, and other uninhabited buildings, where it continues during the day, and leaves its haunts in the twilight in quest of prey. It has obtained the name Screech Owl from its cries, repeated at intervals, and rendered loud and frightful from the stillness of the night. During its repose it makes a blowing hissing noise, resembling the snoring of a man. It makes no nest, but deposits its eggs in the holes of walls, and lays five or six, of a whitish colour. It feeds on mice and small birds, swallowing them whole, and afterwards emitting the bones, feathers, and other indigestible parts, at its mouth, in the form of small round cakes or pellets, which are often found in the empty buildings it frequents.

THE TAWNY OWL

Common Brown Ivy Owl, or Howlet

(*Strix Stridula*, Linn.—*Le Chat-huant*, Buff.)

This bird is about the size of the last. The bill is white: eyes dark blue: the radiated feathers round the eyes are white, finely streaked with brown; the head, neck, back, wing coverts and scapulars, are tawny brown, finely powdered and spotted with dark brown and black; on the wing coverts and scapulars, are several large white spots, regularly placed, so as to form three rows; the quill feathers are marked with alternate bars of light and dark brown; the breast and belly are pale yellow, marked with narrow dark streaks pointing downwards, and crossed with others of the same: the legs are feathered down to the toes; the claws large, much hooked, and white. This species is found in various parts of Europe; it frequents woods, and builds its nest in the hollows of trees. The Tawny Owl and Brown Owl have by the older authors been described as a distinct species; but Latham, Montagu, and Temminck seem to agree in considering them identical, the differences arising merely from age and sex.

THE LITTLE OWL

(Strix passerina, Linn.—La Chevêche ou Petite Chouette, Buff.)

The length of this bird is about nine and a half inches, breadth twenty-one and a half, and weight four ounces: the bill is light horn colour; irides pale yellow; orbits black, and a patch or streak of that colour passes from underneath the eye to the beak. The circular feathers on the face are white, mixed or faintly streaked with pale brown, and surrounded with a border of black, somewhat divided by small spots of white; the head and neck are spotted with pale brown and white; breast and belly white, streaked and patched with various-sized spots of light brown; legs and vent white; back, wings, and tail brown, somewhat inclining to olive, and distinctly marked with white spots. The legs and feet are covered with soft feathers down to the claws. It frequents rocks, caverns, and ruined buildings, makes its rudely constructed nest in the most retired places, and lays four or five eggs, spotted with white and yellow. It sees better in the day-time than other nocturnal birds, and gives chase to small birds on the wing; it likewise feeds on mice: it is said to pluck the birds before it eats them, in which it differs from almost all other Owls. It would appear from the accounts of ornithologists that this bird is seldom seen in Britain. Temminck says it is found in almost every country in Europe, but never farther north than the 55th degree of latitude. The drawing from which our cut was engraved, was taken from a specimen shot at Widdrington, January 1813, and we feel much obliged to Mr R. R. Wingate, of Newcastle, for his drawing, and the aid it affords us, to give a correct representation of this bird.

THE SCOPS EARED OWL

(Strix Scops, Linn.—Le Scops, ou petit Duc, Buff.)

This is the smallest of the Owl kind in this country; its bill is brown at the base, and paler at the tip; irides light yellow. The upper plumage appears brown, the under grey, but on nearer inspection the whole is prettily variegated with white spots, streaks, and bars of dusky brown, rufous and yellow, and almost every feather is speckled with white, brown, and grey; the circular feathers on the face are powdered with brown; the neck, head, and ear feathers, are much the same, but more distinctly marked with bars, streaks, and spots of white, yellow and brown; the back feathers and greater coverts of the wings are barred, streaked, and speckled with the same colours, but on their outer margins are patched with spots of white; the greater quills are transversely barred on their outer webs with white and freckled brown, and barred on the inner webs to their tips with the latter colour; the tail is barred nearly in the same way. The legs are covered to the toes with yellowish soft feathers, and are also brown. The stuffed specimen of this rare and curious little bird, from which our figure and description were taken, was sent to the author by Mr Charles Fothergill, late of York: another is now in the museum of P. J. Selby, Esq. of Twizell House, Northumberland. There is also a very fine specimen in the cabinet of the Hon. Mr Liddell, of Ravensworth Castle.

THE ASH-COLOURED SHRIKE
Greater Butcher Bird
(Lanius Excubitor, Linn.*—La Pie-Grièche grise,* Buff.*)*

The length is about ten inches. Its bill is black, and furnished with bristles at the base: the upper parts of its plumage pale blue ash; under parts white; a black stripe passes through each eye; the greater quills are black, with a large white spot at the base, forming a bar of colour across the wing; the lesser quills are white at the tips; the scapulars white; the two middle feathers of the tail black; the next on each side are white at the ends, gradually increasing to the outermost, which are nearly all white; the whole, when the tail is spread, forms a large oval of black; the legs are black. The female differs little from the male; she lays six eggs, of a dull olive green, spotted at the end with black.

This bird is rarely found in the cultivated parts of the country, preferring mountainous wilds, among furze and thorny thickets. Buffon says it is common in France, where it continues all the year: it is met with likewise in Russia, and various parts of Europe; it preys on small birds, which it seizes by the throat, and, after strangling, fixes them on a sharp thorn, and tears them in pieces with its bill. Pennant observes, that when kept in a cage, it sticks its food against the wires before it will eat it. It is said to imitate the notes of the smaller singing birds, thereby drawing them near its haunts, in order more securely to seize them.

The foregoing figure and description were taken from a very fine specimen, for which this work is indebted to the late Major H. F. Gibson, of the 4th dragoons.

THE RED-BACKED SHRIKE

Flusher, or Lesser Butcher Bird

(Lanius Collurio, Linn.—*L'Ecorcheur,* Buff.*)*

This bird is less than the last, being seven inches and three-quarters long, breadth twelve inches and a quarter. The bill is black; irides hazel; the head and lower part of the back light grey; the upper part of the back and coverts of the wings are bright rusty red; the breast, belly, and sides of a fine pale rose or bloom colour; throat white; a stroke of black passes from the bill through each eye; the two middle feathers of the tail are black, the others white at the base; the quills are brown; the legs black.

The female is somewhat larger than the male; the head is rust-colour, mixed with grey; the breast, belly, and sides dirty white; tail deep brown; the exterior web of the outer feathers white. It builds in hedges or low bushes and lays six white eggs, marked with a reddish brown circle towards the larger end.

The manners of this species are similar to those of the last: it frequently preys on young birds, which it takes in the nest; it likewise feeds on grasshoppers, beetles, and other insects. It also is said to imitate the notes of other birds, in order the more surely to decoy them. When sitting on the nest, the female soon discovers herself at the approach of any person, by her loud and violent outcries.

THE WOODCHAT

(Lanius rufus, Linn.—*La Pie-grièche rousse,* Buff.*)*

Under this title we have introduced the figure of a Shrike which we received from Mr William Proctor, of Auton Stile, Durham. It was shot by him, expressly for this work, on the 10th September, 1824. The length seven inches; breadth eleven; weight rather exceeding an ounce. The bill is dark brown, tinged with lead colour, distinctly notched, and beset with bristles at the base; irides dark hazel; brow dull light brown; the head and upper parts of the body reddish or rusty brown; each feather fringed with a lighter colour, and barred in the middle with black curved or waved lines; the auriculars are deeper brown, and spotted or barred with black; the lower part of the back and rump are of a paler shade than the back; the tail coverts are rusty red, the tail is nearly the same colour; the two middle feathers plain, the two outer ones edged with dull white; the rest have a black spot near the ends, and are tipped with white; the greater coverts and secondaries are deep brown, black in the

middle, with pale edges, and tips white; the primaries are much the same, but of a darker cast; the under parts are sullied white, delicately barred on the breast and sides, with dark brown; the thighs mottled the same; the legs dark lead blue. The gizzard was full of the remains of insects, such as the legs of earwigs and beetles.

There has been much difference of opinion, since the time of Edwards, respecting the Woodchat. Buffon supposes it a variety of the Red-backed Shrike. Pennant, Latham, and Montagu give it a place as a distinct species; so does Temminck, but this country is not mentioned by him as one of its habitats, and we understand Mr Selby excludes it from our Fauna, no instance of its capture or appearance in Britain being upon record. We give the figure therefore, rather with the view of assisting naturalists, than of offering any decided opinion of our own.

THE RAVEN

Great Corbie Crow

(Corvus Corax, Linn.—*Le Corbeau*, Buff.*)*

Is the largest bird of the Pie kind; the length is above two feet; breadth four. The female is somewhat less. The bill is strong, and thick at the base, measuring somewhat more than two inches and a half in length, and covered with strong hairs or bristles, which extend above half its length, covering the nostrils: the general colour of the upper parts is a fine glossy black, reflecting a blue tint in particular lights; the under parts are duller, and of a dusky hue.

The Raven is well known in all parts of the world, and in times of ignorance and superstition, was regarded as a bird of ill omen, announcing by its croaking, impending calamities: Of such vast importance was it considered, that the various modulations of its voice were studied with the most careful attention, and were made use of by designing men to mislead the ignorant and credulous. It is a very long-lived bird, and is supposed sometimes to live a century or more. It is fond of carrion, which it scents at a great distance; it will destroy rabbits, young ducks, and chickens; and has been known to seize on young lambs, and even sheep, when sick or weak, and pick out their eyes while yet alive: it will suck the eggs of other birds; it feeds also on earthworms, reptiles, and even shellfish, when urged by hunger. It may be rendered very tame and familiar, and has often been taught to pronounce a variety of words: it is a crafty bird, and will frequently pick up things of value, such as rings, money, &c. and carry them to its hiding place. They build early in the spring, in trees and the holes of rocks, laying five or six eggs, of a pale bluish green, spotted with brown. The female sits about twenty days, and is constantly attended by the male, who not only provides her with abundance of food, but relieves her in turn, and takes her place in the nest.

THE CROW

Carrion crow, Black-nebbed or Midden Crow
(Corvus Corone, Linn.—*La Corneille noire,* Buff.)

Is similar to the Raven in its habits, colour, and external appearance. Length about eighteen inches; breadth three feet. The glossy feathers of the upper plumage have a burnished look, excepting on their edges, which are dull, and form a border to each. This species is more numerous and as widely spread as the Raven; they live mostly in woods; build their nests in trees; and lay five or six eggs, much like those of the Raven. They feed on putrid flesh, and garbage of all sorts; likewise on eggs, shellfish, worms, and insects.

These wary birds live in pairs, and are commonly seen together flying at a great height, out of the reach of the gun, while they are prowling over the country in search of their food, which, with penetrating eye, and acute scent, they discover afar off. They pluck the feathers off the dead birds, toss them aside, and then pick the flesh from the bones. In winter they take shelter from the extremity of the weather, in the hollows of rocky precipices.

THE HOODED CROW

(Corvus Cornix, Linn.—La Corneille Mantelée, Buff.)

Is somewhat larger and more bulky than the Rook, measuring twenty-two inches in length. The bill is black, and two inches long; the head, fore part of the neck, wings, and tail black; the back and all the under parts are of a pale ash; the legs black.

These birds arrive with the Woodcock, and on their first coming frequent the shores of rivers. They depart in the spring, but they do not all leave us, as they have been seen during the summer months, in the northern quarters of our island, where they frequent the mountainous parts of the country, and breed in the pines. In the Shetland islands they are the only species of Crow met with, and breed in the rocky cliffs on the sea coast. There, and in more northern parts of the world they continue the whole year, and subsist on sea-worms, shellfish, and other marine productions. With us they are seen to mix with, and to feed in the same manner as the Crow. During the breeding season they live in pairs, lay six eggs, seldom more than two or three of which are prolific. They are much attached to their offspring.

THE ROOK

(Corvus frugilegus, Linn.—*Le Freux,* Buff.)

Is about the size of the Carrion Crow, and in its figure very much resembles it. The base of the bill and nostrils, as far as the eyes, is covered with a rough scabrous skin, in which it differs from all the rest of the genus. Rooks are fond of the erucæ of the hedge-chafer, or chestnut-brown beetle, for which they search with indefatigable pains. They are often accused of feeding on the corn just after it has been sown, and various contrivances have been made both to kill and frighten them away; but, in our estimation, the advantages derived from the destruction which they make among grubs, larvæ, worms, and noxious insects, greatly overpay the injury done to the future harvest, by the small quantity of corn they may destroy in searching after their favourite food. They are gregarious, and fly in immense flocks morning and evening to and from their roosting places in quest of food. During the breeding time they are jealous and watchful, and will rob each other when they can.

They live together in large societies, and build close to each other in trees, frequently in the midst of large and populous towns. These rookeries, however, are often the scenes of bitter contests; the newcomers are frequently driven away by the old inhabitants, their half-built nests torn in pieces, and the unfortunate couple forced to begin their work anew in some more undisturbed situation: of this we had a remarkable instance in Newcastle. In the year 1788, a pair of Rooks, after an unsuccessful attempt to establish themselves in a rookery at no great distance from the Exchange, were compelled to abandon the attempt. They took refuge on the spire of that building, and although constantly interrupted by other Rooks, built their nest on the top of the vane, and brought forth their young, undisturbed by the noise of the populace below them; the nest and its inhabitants turning about with every change of the wind.

THE JACK-DAW

(Corvus Monedula, Linn.—*Le Choucas,* Buff.*)*

This bird is considerably less than the Rook, being only thirteen inches in length, and about twenty-eight in breadth. The bill is black: eyes white; the hinder part of the head and neck hoary grey; the rest of the plumage is of a fine glossy black above; beneath dusky; the legs are black.

The Daw is very common in England, and remains with us the whole year: in other countries, such as France and various parts of Germany, it is migratory. They frequent churches, old towers, and ruins, in great flocks, where they build: the female lays five or six eggs, paler than those of the Crow, and smaller. They rarely build in trees: in Hampshire they sometimes breed in rabbit holes. They are easily tamed, and may be taught to pronounce several words: they will conceal part of their food, and with it small pieces of money, or toys. They feed on insects, grain, fruit, and small pieces of flesh, and will also eat eggs.

There is a variety of the Daw found in Switzerland, having a white collar round its neck. In Norway and even in this country, individuals have been seen perfectly white.

46

THE CHOUGH
Red-legged Crow
(*Corvus Graculus*, Linn.—*Le Coracias*, Buff.)

This bird is about the weight of the Jack-Daw, but of a taller and longer shape. The bill is long, curved, sharp at the tip, and of a bright red; the iris is composed of two circles, the outer red, the inner light blue; the eyelids are red; the plumage is altogether of a purplish violet black; legs red like the bill; claws large, hooked, and black. It builds on high cliffs, by the sea side, lays four or five eggs, spotted with yellow, and chiefly frequents the coasts of Devonshire and Cornwall, and likewise many parts of Wales: some are found on the cliffs of Dover, and a few in Scotland. In a wild state it feeds chiefly on insects and berries. It is easily tamed, becomes extremely docile, and is very fond of being caressed, by those to whom it shows an attachment, but its shrill notes and mischievous qualities render it sometimes a troublesome inmate. It also becomes bold and pugnacious, and resents an affront with violence and effect, by both bill and claws. It has a great aversion to strangers. Like the tame Jack-Daw it is fond of glittering objects, and is equally mischievous, active, and restless. It examines everything, and is perpetually in search of insects. It soon learns to eat raw or dressed meat, bread, and soft grain, but will not eat common worms.

THE MAGPIE

Pianet

(Corvus Pica, Linn.—La Pie, Buff.)

Length about eighteen inches. Bill strong and black; eyes hazel; head, neck, back, breast, and tail coverts deep black, forming a fine contrast with the snowy whiteness of the under parts and scapulars; the neck feathers are long, as are also those on the back, which extend towards the rump, leaving only a small space, of ash-grey, between them and the tail coverts; the plumage in general is glossed with green, purple, and blue, which catch the eye in different lights, and are particularly resplendent on the tail, which is very long, and rather wedge-shaped; vent, under tail-coverts, thighs, and legs black: on the throat and part of the neck the feathers are mixed with others, resembling strong whitish hairs.

This bird is everywhere common in England; and is likewise found in various parts of the Continent, but not so far north as Lapland, nor farther south than Italy: it is met with in America, but not commonly, and is migratory there. Like the Crow it is omnivorous. They make their nest with great art, leaving a hole in the side for admittance, and covering the whole upper part with an interweaving of thorny twigs, closely entangled, thereby securing a retreat from the rude attacks of other birds: the inside is furnished with a sort of mattress, composed of wool and other soft materials, on which the young repose: the female lays seven or eight eggs, pale green, spotted with black.

The Magpie is crafty and familiar, and may be taught to pronounce words, and even short sentences, and will imitate any particular noise. It is addicted, like other birds of its kind, to stealing and hoarding. It is smaller than the Jack-Daw, and its wings are shorter in proportion; accordingly its flight is not so lofty, nor so well sustained: it never undertakes long journeys, but flies only from tree to tree, at moderate distances.

THE JAY

(Corvus glandarius, Linn.—Le Geai, Buff.)

This beautiful bird is not more than thirteen inches in length. Its bill is black; eyes white; the feathers on the forehead are white, streaked with black, and form a tuft which it can erect and depress at will; the chin is white, and from the corners of the bill on each side proceeds a broad streak of black, which passes under the eye; the hinder part of the head, the neck, and back, are of a cinnamon colour; breast the same, but lighter; lesser wing coverts bay; the belly and vent almost white; the greater wing coverts are elegantly barred with black, fine pale blue, and white alternately; the greater quills are black, with pale edges, the bases of some of them white; lesser quills black; those next the body chestnut; the rump is white; tail black, with pale brown edges; legs dirty pale brown.

The Jay is common in Great Britain, and is found in various parts of Europe. It builds in woods, and makes an artless nest of sticks, fibres, and slender twigs: lays five or six eggs, ash grey, mixed with green, and faintly spotted with brown. Pennant observes that the young ones continue with their parents till the following spring, when they separate to form new pairs.

They live on acorns, nuts, seeds, and fruits; will eat eggs, and sometimes destroy young birds in the absence of the old ones. When domesticated, they may be very familiar, and will imitate a variety of words and sounds. They sometimes assemble in great numbers early in the spring, and seem to hold a conference, probably for the purpose of fixing upon the districts they are to occupy: to hear them is truly curious; while some gabble, shout, or whistle, others with a raucous voice, seem to command attention: the noise made on these occasions may be aptly compared to that of a distant meeting of disorderly drunken persons.

THE CHATTERER
Silk Tail, or Waxen Chatterer
(Ampelis Garrulus, Linn.*—Le Jaseur de Boheme,* Buff.*)*

This beautiful bird is about eight inches in length. Its bill is black, and has a small notch at the end; the eyes, which are black and shining, are placed in a band of black, passing from the base of the bill to the hinder part of the head; throat black; the feathers on the head long, forming a crest; all the upper parts of the body are of a reddish ash; breast and belly inclining to purple; the vent and tail coverts in some, nearly white; in others, the former reddish chestnut, the latter ash grey: the tail feathers are black, tipped with pale yellow; the quills black, the third and fourth tipped on their outer edges with white, the five following with straw colour, but in some bright yellow; the secondaries are tipped with white, each being pointed with a flat horny substance of a bright vermillion. These appendages vary in different subjects; one in our possession, had eight on one wing and six on the other. The legs are short and black. The female has only four or five of the second quills tipped with the red cartilaginous appendages, and the young birds previous to their first moult are without them altogether.

This rare bird visits our island only at uncertain intervals. In the years 1790, 1791, and 1803, several were taken in Northumberland and Durham, in the month of November. Their summer residence is the northern parts of Europe, within the Arctic circle, whence they spread themselves into other countries, where they remain during winter, and return in the spring to their usual haunts. Their general food is berries and insects: one which we saw in a state of captivity was fed chiefly with hawthorn and ivy berries, but from the difficulty of providing it with this food, it soon died. Its breeding place is not well ascertained.

THE GOLDEN ORIOLE

Golden Thrush

(Oriolus Galbula, Linn.—*Le Loriot*, Buff.*)*

The Golden Oriole is about the size and shape of the Blackbird, but its bill is somewhat larger and stronger; it is rather elevated and arched, and slightly notched at the tip, and, as well as the irides, is reddish; a patch or stroke of black covers the space between the corners of the mouth and the eyes, and this spot is thinly beset with a few hairs. The whole plumage, excepting the wings and tail, is pure yellow; the two latter are black, but are marked as follows: the edge of the wing at the alula spuria, is yellow, with a spot or patch of that colour below, on the tips of the first series of the primary quills, or second bastard wing. The first quill of the primaries is remarkably short, the second shorter than the third, and both the former are wholly black; the third and fourth are slightly edged with yellow on part of their outer webs; all the rest of the quills are more or less slightly tipped with yellow, and glossed like satin on their undersides. The tail consists of twelve feathers; the two middle ones black, slightly tipped with yellow; all the rest more or less deeply marked with that colour, from their tips upwards. The legs are short, and, as well as the toes, black, with the undersides wide or spread out, and having rather a coarse appearance; claws hooked and strong. The plumage of the female differs from that of the male. Where he is yellow, she is of a dull olive green; her wing coverts, secondary quills, and upper parts of the tail feathers, partake of the same colour, but are much darker; the quills and lower ends of the tail feathers are dusky, and, as well as the former, are all tipped, less or more, with pale dull yellow. These birds are rare visitants in this country; but they are often met with in the southern parts of Europe in the summer season.

THE STARLING

Stare

(Sturnus vulgaris, Linn.—*L'Etourneau,* Buff.*)*

Length somewhat less than nine inches. The bill is straight, sharp-pointed, and of a yellowish brown; in old birds deep yellow; the nostrils are surrounded by a prominent rim; the eyes are brown; the whole plumage dark, glossed with green, blue, purple, and copper, but each feather is marked at the end with a pale yellow spot; the wing coverts are edged with yellowish brown; the quill and tail feathers dusky, with light edges: the legs are reddish brown.

From the striking similarity, both in form and manners, observable in the Starling, and those more immediately preceding, we have no scruple in removing it from the usual place, as it evidently forms a connecting link between them, and in a variety of points seems equally allied to both. Few birds are more generally known than the Starling, it being an inhabitant of almost every climate; and as it is a familiar bird, and easily trained in a state of captivity, its habits have been more frequently observed than those of most other birds. They make an artless nest in the hollows of trees, rocks, or old walls, and sometimes in cliffs overhanging the sea: lay four or five eggs, of a pale greenish ash: the young are dusky brown till the first moult. In the autumn they fly in vast flocks, and may be known at a great distance, by their whirling mode of flight, which Buffon compares to a sort of vortex, in which the collective body performs a uniform circular revolution, and at the same time continues to make a progressive advance. The evening is the time when the Starlings assemble in the greatest numbers, and, it is said, betake themselves to the fens and marshes, where they roost among the reeds. Their principal food consists of worms, snails, and caterpillars; they likewise break and suck the eggs of other birds, and eat various kinds of grain, seeds, and berries, and are said to be particularly fond of cherries.

THE MISSEL THRUSH
Missel Bird or Shrite
(Turdus viscivorus, Linn. —*La Drainè,* Buff.*)*

Length eleven inches and three quarters, breadth above eighteen. The bill is dusky; the base of the lower mandible yellow; the eyes hazel; the head, back, and lesser coverts of the wings olive brown, the latter tipped with dull brownish white; the lower part of the back and rump tinged with yellowish brown and ash; the cheeks are yellowish white, spotted with brown; the breast and belly pale yellow, marked with larger spots of very dark brown; quills brown, with pale edges; tail feathers the same, the three outermost tipped with white: the legs are yellow; claws black; builds mostly on low trees, or on high bushes, and lays four or five eggs of a greenish blue, marked with reddish spots. The nest is made of moss, leaves, &c. lined with dry grass, and strengthened on the outside with small twigs. This species begins to sing early, often on the turn of the year in blowing showery weather, whence, in some places it is called the Stormcock. Its note of anger is very loud and harsh, between a chatter and a shriek, which accounts for some of its names. It feeds on various kinds of berries, particularly those of the mountain ash, and the mistletoe. It was formerly believed that the latter plant was only propagated by the seed which passed the digestive organs of this bird, whence arose the proverb *'Turdus malum sibi cacat'*[1]; it likewise feeds on caterpillars and insects, with which it also feeds its young. This bird is found in various parts of Europe, and is said to be migratory in some places, but continues in England the whole year, and frequently has two broods.

---

1 *Literally: 'The thrush defecates its own destruction.' The digested mistletoe berries can produce the adhesive substance birdlime, used for trapping birds.*

THE THROSTLE
Thrush, Grey Bird, or Mavis
(Turdus Musicus, Linn.—*La Grive,* Buff.*)*

This is larger than the Redwing, but much less than the Missel, to which it bears a strong resemblance both in form and colours. A small notch is observable at the end of the bill, which belongs to this and every bird of the Thrush kind: throat white, and the spots on the breast more regularly formed than those of the Missel Thrush, and conical; inside of the wings and mouth yellow, as are also the legs; claws strong and black.

The Throstle is distinguished among our singing birds by the clearness and fullness of its note; it charms us not only with the sweetness, but the variety of its song, which it begins early in the spring, and continues during part of the summer.

The female builds her nest generally in bushes; it is composed of dried grass, with a little earth or clay intermixed, and lined with rotten wood; she lays five or six eggs, of a pale blue colour, marked with dusky spots.

Although this species is not considered with us as migratory, it has, nevertheless, been observed in some places in great numbers during the spring and summer, where not one was to be seen in the winter, which has induced an opinion that they either shift their quarters entirely, or take shelter in the more retired parts of the woods. The Throstle is migratory in France: Buffon says that it appears in Burgundy about the end of September, before the Redwing and Fieldfare, and that it feeds upon the ripe grapes, and sometimes does much damage to the vineyards. The females of all the Thrush kind are very similar to the males, and differ chiefly in a lesser degree of brilliancy in the colours.

THE FIELDFARE

(Turdus pilaris, Linn.—La Litorne, ou Tourdelle, Buff.)

This is somewhat less than the Missel Thrush; length ten inches. The bill is yellow; each corner of the mouth is furnished with a few black bristly hairs; eyes light brown; the top of the head, hinder part of the neck, the lower part of the back and the rump are light bluish ash, the former spotted with black; the back and coverts of the wings are deep hoary brown; the throat and breast yellow, regularly spotted with black; the belly and thighs yellowish white; tail brown, inclining to black; the legs dusky yellowish brown; in young birds yellow.

We have seen a variety of this bird, of which the head and neck were yellowish white; the rest of the body nearly of the same colour, mixed with a few brown feathers; the spots on the breast were faint and indistinct; the quill feathers perfectly white, except one or two on each side, which were brown; the tail was marked in a similar manner.

The Fieldfare is only a visitant in this island, making its appearance about the beginning of October, in order to avoid the rigorous winters of the north, whence it sometimes comes in great flocks, according to the severity of the season, and leaves us about the latter end of February or the beginning of March, and retires to Russia, Sweden, Norway, and as far as Siberia and Kamtschatka. Buffon observes that they do not arrive in France till the beginning of December, that they assemble in flocks of two or three thousand, and feed on haws and other berries; they likewise eat worms, of various kinds.

Fieldfares seem more sociable than the Throstles or the Missels: they are sometimes seen singly, but in general form very large flocks, and fly in a body; and though they often spread through the fields in search of food, they seldom lose sight of each other, but, when alarmed, fly off, and collect upon the same tree.

THE REDWING

Swinepipe, or Wind Thrush

(Turdus Iliacus, Linn. —*Le Mauvis,* Buff*.)*

Is about eight inches in length. Bill dark brown; eyes deep hazel; plumage in general similar to that of the Thrush, but a white streak over the eye distinguishes it from that bird; belly not quite so much spotted, sides of the body and the feathers under the wings tinged with red, which is its peculiar characteristic; whence also its name.

These birds make their appearance a few days before the Fieldfare,[1] and are generally seen with them after their arrival; they frequent the same places, eat the same food, and are very similar to them in manners. Like the Fieldfare, they leave us in the spring, for which reason their song is almost unknown to us, but it is said to be very pleasing. In Sweden they perch on high trees in the forests, and have a fine note in the breeding season. The female builds her nest in low bushes or hedges, and lays six eggs, of a greenish blue colour, spotted with black.[2]

1 *A Redwing was taken up November 7th, 1785, at six o'clock in the morning, which, on its approach to land, had flown against the lighthouse at Tynemouth, and was so stunned that it fell to the ground and died soon after; the light most probably had attracted its attention. [Bewick's note]*

2 *This and the former are delicate eating: the Romans held them in such estimation that they kept thousands of them together in aviaries, and fed them with a sort of paste made of bruised figs and flour, and various other kind of food, to improve the delicacy and flavour of their flesh: these aviaries were so contrived as to admit light barely sufficient to direct them to their food; every object which might tend to remind them of their former liberty was carefully kept out of sight, such as the fields, the woods, the birds, or whatever might disturb the repose necessary to their improvement. Under this management these birds fattened, to the great profit of their proprietors, who sold them to the Roman epicures for three denarii, or about two shillings sterling each. [Bewick's note]*

THE BLACKBIRD
Black Ouzel
(Turdus Merula, Linn.—*Le Merle*, Buff)

The length of the Blackbird is generally about ten inches. Its plumage is altogether black; the bill, inside of the mouth, and edges of the eyelids are yellow, as are also the soles of the feet; legs dirty yellow. The female is mostly deep brown, inclining to rust colour on the breast and belly; bill dusky, legs brown; her song is also very different, so that she has sometimes been mistaken for a bird of a different species.

The males, during the first year, resemble the females so much as not easily to be distinguished from them; but after that, they assume the yellow bill, and other distinguishing marks of their sex. The Blackbird is a solitary bird, frequenting woods and thickets, chiefly evergreens, especially where there are perennial springs, which together afford it both shelter and subsistence. They feed on berries, fruits, insects, and worms; but never fly in flocks like Thrushes; they pair early, and begin to warble nearly as soon as any other songsters of the grove. They build in bushes or low trees, and lay four or five eggs, of a bluish green, marked irregularly with dusky spots. The young birds are easily tamed, and may be taught to whistle a variety of tunes. They are restless and timorous birds, easily alarmed, and difficult of access; but they readily suffer themselves to be caught with birdlime, nooses, and all sorts of snares. They are never kept in aviaries, but generally in cages apart; for, when shut up with other birds, they pursue and harass their companions unceasingly. In some counties of England this bird is called simply the Ouzel.

THE RING OUZEL

(Turdus torquatus, Linn.—*Le Merle à Plastron Blanc,* Buff.*)*

This bird very much resembles the Blackbird: its general colour is dull black; each feather margined with ash grey; the bill is dusky; corners of the mouth and inside yellow; eyes hazel; the breast is distinguished by a crescent of pure white, which almost surrounds the neck, and from which it derives its name: the legs are dusky brown. The female differs in having the crescent on the breast much less conspicuous, and, in some birds, wholly wanting, which has caused some authors to consider it as a different species, under the name of the Rock Ouzel.

Ring Ouzels are found in various parts of this kingdom, chiefly in the wilder and more mountainous districts: with this exception, their habits are similar to those of the Blackbird; the female builds her nest in the same manner, and in similar situations, and lays four or five eggs of the same colour: they feed on insects and berries of various kinds, are fond of grapes, and, Buffon observes, during the season of vintage are generally fat, and at that time are esteemed delicious eating. The same author says, that in France they are migratory. In some parts of this kingdom they have been observed to change places, particularly in Hampshire, where they are known generally to stay not more than a fortnight at one time. The foregoing representation was taken from one killed near Bedlington, Northumberland.

THE CUCKOO

Gowk

(*Cuculus canorus*, Linn.—*Le Coucou*, Buff.)

Length fourteen inches; breadth twenty-five: the bill is black and somewhat bent; eyes yellow; inside of the mouth red; its head, neck, back, and wing coverts pale blue, darkest on the head and back, and palest on the fore part of the neck and rump; breast and belly white, elegantly crossed with wavy bars of black; the quill feathers are dusky, their inner webs marked with large oval white spots; the tail is long; the two middle feathers black, with white tips; the others dusky, marked with alternate spots of white on each side of the shaft: legs short and yellow; toes, two forward, two backward; the outer one capable of being directed forward or backward at pleasure; claws white.

The Cuckoo visits us early in spring; the well-known cry of the male is commonly heard about the middle of April, and ceases at the end of June: its stay is short, the old birds quitting this country early in July.

Whether Cuckoos pair is not known, but it is certain that they build no nest; and what is more extraordinary, the female deposits one of her eggs (of which she lays from four to six during the season) in the nest of some other bird, by whom it is hatched. The nest usually chosen for this purpose is that of the Titlark, Hedge Sparrow, Water Wagtail, Yellow-hammer, Green Linnet, or Whinchat, the two first being generally preferred.

We owe the first satisfactory account of the singular economy of this bird, in the disposal of its egg, to Mr Edward Jenner, afterwards Dr Jenner, the illustrious discoverer of vaccination. The following being the result of repeated observations and experiments, accurately made by himself, we shall detail it as nearly as possible in his own words.

During the four or five days occupied by the Hedge Sparrow (or any bird that happens to be selected) in laying, the Cuckoo deposits her egg among the rest, leaving the future care of it entirely to the Hedge Sparrow. This intrusion often occasions discomposure, for the Hedge Sparrow, whilst sitting, not only throws out some of her own eggs, but injures others, so that not more than two or three of them are hatched along with that of the Cuckoo, and what is very remarkable, she never throws out or injures the egg of the intruder. When she has disengaged the young Cuckoo and her own offspring from the shell, her young ones, and any of her eggs that remain unhatched, are soon turned out by the young Cuckoo, who becomes the sole object of the care of its foster parents. The young birds are not previously killed, nor the eggs demolished, but all are left to perish together, entangled in the bush which contains the nest, or lying on the ground near it. The mode of accomplishing the ejectment is curious: The Cuckoo, very soon after being hatched, and while it is yet blind, contrives with its rump and wings to get the Hedge Sparrow, or the egg, upon its back, and making a lodgement for its burden by elevating its elbows, clambers backwards with it up the side of the nest, till it reaches the top, where resting for a moment, it throws off its load with a jerk, and quite disengages it from the nest; after remaining a short time in this situation, and feeling about with the extremities of its wings, as if to be convinced that

the business has been properly executed, it drops into the nest again. Nature seems to have provided, even in the formation of the Cuckoo, for the exercise of this peculiar instinct, for unlike other newly hatched birds, its back from the scapulæ downwards, is very broad, with a considerable depression in the middle, as if for the purpose of giving a more secure lodgement to the egg, or the young bird, while the intruder is removing either from the nest; when about twelve days old, this cavity is filled up, and the back assumes the shape of nestling birds in general. The smallness of the Cuckoo's egg is another circumstance deserving attention in this surprising transaction; in size and appearance, it differs little from the egg of the Skylark and Titlark, though the disparity of bulk of the birds be very great: In short, everything conspires, as might be expected, to render perfect the design which is to be accomplished by the seemingly unnatural propensity of this bird.

Young Cuckoos differ so much in plumage from the old, that they have sometimes been mistaken for a different species. In the young birds, the bill, legs, and tail, are nearly the same as those of the old; iris blue; throat, neck, breast, and belly, elegantly barred with dark brown, on a light ground; the back is lead grey, mixed with brown, and faintly barred with white; the tail feathers irregularly marked with black, light brown, and white, and tipped with white; legs yellow. They continue three weeks in the nest before they fly, and the foster parents feed them five weeks after this period. Their growth is very rapid. They migrate probably in succession, about the end of August, or beginning of September, and undergo their first moult during their absence.

THE BLACK WOODPECKER

(Picus martius, Linn.—*Le Pic noir,* Buff.*)*

This scarce bird is the largest of the British Woodpeckers, being about seventeen inches in length, bill nearly two and a half, of a horn colour, and pale yellow on the sides; irides also pale yellow; the crown of the head is crimson, and the feathers elongated to the nape; the quills are brown, and all the rest of the plumage dull black; the legs are lead grey, having the fore part covered with feathers half their length.

The female differs from the male, the hinder part of her head only being red, and in some specimens, the red is entirely wanting; the black parts of her plumage are also duller. They form their nest in the deep hollows of old trees, and like the rest of the genus lay two or three white eggs.

THE GREEN WOODPECKER

Woodspite, High-hoe, Hew-hole, or Pick-a-tree

(Picus viridis, Linn.—Le Pic verd, Buff.)

This is the second in size of the British Woodpeckers, being thirteen inches in length. The bill is two inches long, triangular, and of a dark horn colour; the tongue towards the tip is furnished with numerous fibres, projecting transversely, of the size of minute hairs; the outer circle of the eye is white, surrounding another of red; top of the head bright crimson, which extends down the hinder part of the neck, ending in a point behind; the eye is surrounded by a black space; and from each corner of the bill runs a crimson streak pointing downwards; back and wing coverts olive green; rump yellow; the quill feathers are dusky, barred on the outer web with black and white; the bastard wing spotted with white; sides of the head and under parts of the body white, slightly tinged with green; the tail is marked with bars like the wings; legs greenish. The female differs from the male in not having the red mark from the corner of the mouth; she makes her nest in the hollow of a tree, fifteen or twenty feet from the ground. Buffon observes that both male and female labour by turns in boring through the sound part of the wood, sometimes to a considerable depth, until they penetrate to that which is decayed and rotten, where she lays five or six eggs, of a greenish colour, marked with small black spots.

The Green Woodpecker is seen more frequently on the ground than the other kinds, particularly where there are anthills. It inserts its long tongue into the holes through which the ants issue, and draws out ants in abundance. Sometimes, with its feet and bill, it makes a breach in the nest, and devours them at its ease, together with their eggs. The young ones climb up and down the trees before they are able to fly: they roost very early, and repose in their holes till day.

THE PIED WOODPECKER

Greater Spotted Woodpecker, or Witwall

(Picus major, Linn.—L'Epeiche, ou le Pic varié, Buff.)

Length somewhat more than nine inches. The bill is of a dark horn colour, very strong at the base, and exceedingly sharp at the end; the upper and under sides formed by high-pointed ridges, which run along the middle of each; the eyes are reddish, encircled with a large white spot, which extends to the back part of the head, on which is a spot of crimson; the forehead is buff; the top of the head black; on the back part of the neck are two white spots, separated by a line of black; the scapulars and tips of the wing coverts white; the rest of the plumage on the upper part of the body black; the tail is black, the outer feathers marked with white spots; the throat, breast, and part of the belly yellowish white; the vent and lower part of the belly crimson; legs and feet lead grey. The female has not the red spot on the back of the head.

This bird is common in England. Buffon says that it strikes against the trees with brisker and harder blows than the Green Woodpecker. It creeps with great ease in all directions upon the branches of trees, and is with difficulty seen, as it instantly avoids the sight by creeping behind a branch, where it remains concealed.

THE NUTHATCH

Nutjobber, Woodcracker

(Sitta europea, Linn.—La Sittelle ou le Torchepot, Buff.)

The length is near six inches; bill strong, black above, beneath almost white; the eyes hazel; a black stroke passes over each eye, from the bill, extending down the side of the neck as far as the shoulder; all the upper part of the body is of a fine blue grey; the cheeks and chin white; breast and belly of a pale orange; sides marked with streaks of chestnut; quills dusky; the tail is short, the two middle feathers grey, the rest dusky, three of the outermost spotted with white; legs pale yellow; claws large, sharp, and much bent, the back claw very strong; when extended the foot measures one inch and three quarters.

This, like the Woodpecker, frequents woods, and is a shy and solitary bird: the female lays her eggs, which are white, with a few pale brown spots, in holes of trees, frequently in those which have been deserted by the Woodpecker. The nest is fitted up with layers of the very thin flakes or laminæ of the bark of the Scotch fir. During the time of incubation, she is easily driven from her nest, and on being disturbed, hisses like a snake. The Nuthatch feeds on caterpillars, beetles, and various kinds of insects; it likewise eats nuts, and from its expertness in cracking them has obtained its name: having placed a nut fast in a chink, it takes its stand a little above, and striking it with all its force, perforates the shell and picks out the kernel; when disturbed at its work, it very readily removes the nut and flies away with it. In the same way it also breaks into the very hard shells of the stone pine. Like the Woodpecker, it moves up and down the trunks of trees with great facility, in search of food. It does not migrate, but in the winter approaches nearer inhabited places, is sometimes seen in orchards and gardens, and is fond of picking bones.

THE HOOPOE

(Upupa Epops, Linn.—Le Huppe ou Puput, Buff.)

Length twelve inches; breadth nineteen. The bill is about two inches long, black, slender, and somewhat curved; eyes hazel; the tongue very short and triangular; the head is ornamented with a crest, consisting of a double row of feathers, of a pale orange yellow, tipped with black, the highest about two inches in length; the neck is pale reddish brown; breast and belly white, and in young birds marked with various dusky lines pointing downwards; the back, scapulars and wings are crossed with broad bars of black and white; the lesser coverts of the wings light brown; rump white; the tail consists of ten feathers, each marked with white, and when closed, assumes the form of a crescent, the horns pointing downwards: the legs are short and black.

This is the only species of its kind found in this kingdom; and it is not very common with us, being seen only at uncertain periods. The foregoing representation was taken from a very fine one, shot near Bedlington. The sexes differ little in appearance; they moult once a year. The female is said to have two or three broods in the year; she makes no nest, but lays her eggs, generally about four or five in number, in the hollow of a tree, and sometimes in a hole of a wall, or even on the ground. Buffon says, that he has sometimes found a soft lining of moss, wool, or feathers, in the nests of these birds, and supposes that, in this case, they may have used the deserted nest of some other bird. Its food consists chiefly of insects, with the remains of which its nest is sometimes so filled as to become extremely offensive. Its crest usually falls behind on its neck, except when it is surprised or irritated; it then stands erect; and its tail also, as well as its crest, is generally at the same time erected, and spread like a fan.

THE CROSSBILL

Shel-apple

(Loxia Curvirostra, Linn.—*Le Bec Croisé*, Buff.*)*

Is about the size of a Lark, being nearly seven inches in length. It is distinguished by the formation of its bill, the upper and under mandibles curving in opposite directions, and crossing each other near the points: its eyes are hazel; the general colour is reddish, mixed with brown on the upper parts; the under parts are paler, being almost white at the belly and vent; the wings are short, not reaching farther than the tail coverts, and brown; the tail the same, and somewhat forked; legs black. Individuals vary in the colours of their plumage; among a great number hardly two are exactly similar; they likewise vary with the season, and according to the age of the bird. Edwards paints the male of a rose colour, and the female of a yellowish green, mixed more or less with brown. Both sexes appear very different at different times of the year.

The Crossbill is an inhabitant of colder climates, and has been found as far north as Greenland. It breeds in Russia, Sweden, Poland, and Germany, in the mountains of Switzerland, and among the Alps and Pyrenees, whence it migrates in vast flocks into other countries. It sometimes is met with in great numbers in this country, but its visits are not regular, as in some years it is rarely to be seen. Its principal food is said to be the seeds of the pine tree; it is observed to hold the cone in one claw like the Parrot, and when kept in a cage, has all the actions of that bird, climbing, by means of its hooked bill, from the lower to the upper bars of its cage. From its mode of scrambling, and the beauty of its colours, it has been called by some the German Parrot. The female is said to begin to build as early as January; she places her nest under the bare branches of the pine, fixing it with the resinous matter which exudes from that tree, and besmearing it on the outside with the same substance, so that the melted snow or rain cannot penetrate it.

THE PARROT CROSSBILL

(*Loxia pityopsittacus.*—Temm. after Bechstein.)

Our acknowledgements are here due to Sir William Jardine, of Jardine Hall, Bart. for the loan of the preserved specimen from which the above figure was taken. It was shot in Ross-shire, in 1822, and appears to be the same, or nearly so, that Temminck describes under the designation we have given to it. The bill dark horn; irides hazel; the predominant colour of this bird is red, rather clouded on the back, and more or less mixed with green on the breast, belly, and vent; the hinder part of the neck is mixed with dark ash; the wings and tail dusky, each feather distinctly edged either with a pale colour, or with a pale green; the legs and toes dusky; claws hooked, and rather strong. It has been observed before, that scarcely two of these birds are alike in plumage, the crossings of their bills also vary in different individuals, so as to leave us in some doubt, whether this may be a distinct species or not. They chiefly inhabit the countries within the Arctic circle, where the greater number remain to breed. In winter they spread themselves over the great pine forests of Poland, Prussia, and Germany, and return to the north in summer. In France and Holland, it is a bird of passage. Its food is the seeds of the pine and alder.

67

THE PINE GROSBEAK
Greatest Bullfinch
(Loxia Enucleator, Linn.—*Le Dur-bec,* Buff.*)*

Length nine inches. Bill dusky, very stout at the base, and somewhat hooked at the tip: head, neck, breast, rump and sides rose-coloured crimson; back and wing coverts deep brown, each feather edged with pale reddish brown; and the greater and lesser coverts tipped with dull white, forming a bar on the wing; the quills are nearly black, with pale edges; the secondaries the same, but edged with white; the belly and vent are straw-coloured; the tail is marked as the quills, and is somewhat forked; the legs are brown. They are found only in the northern parts of this island and of Europe; are common in various parts of North America, visiting the southern settlements in the winter, and retiring northwards in the summer to breed: like the Crossbill, they frequent pine forests, and feed on the seeds of that tree. They build on trees, at a small distance from the ground, and lay four white eggs, which are hatched in June.

THE BULLFINCH

Alp, or Nope

(Loxia Pyrrhula, Linn.—Le Bouvreuil, Buff.)

The bill is dusky; eyes black; the upper part of the head, the ring round the bill, and the origin of the neck fine glossy black;[1] the back ash grey; breast and belly red; wings and tail black; the upper tail coverts and vent are white; legs dark brown. The female is very like the male, but the colours are less bright, and the under parts of a reddish brown.[2] They are always seen in pairs.

This bird is common in every part of our island, as well as in most parts of Europe; its usual haunts, during summer, are woods and thickets, but in winter it approaches nearer to cultivated grounds, and feeds on seeds, winter berries, &c.; in the spring it frequents gardens, where it is useful in destroying worms which are lodged in the tender buds. The female makes her nest in bushes; it is composed chiefly of moss; she lays five or six eggs, of a dull bluish white, marked at the larger end with dark spots. In a wild state, its note is very simple; but when kept in a cage, its song, though in a subdued tone, is far from unpleasant. Both male and female may be taught to whistle a variety of tunes. They are frequently imported into this country from Germany, where they are taught to articulate, with great distinctness, several words.

1 *Hence in some countries it is called Monk or Pope, and in Scotland it is not improperly denominated Coally-hood.* [Bewick's note]

2 *The Bullfinch sometimes changes its plumage, and becomes wholly black during its confinement, especially when fed with hemp-seed. In the British Museum there is a variety of the Bullfinch entirely white: we have seen others in the same plumage.* [Bewick's note]

THE BUNTING

(Emberiza Miliaria, Linn.—Le Proyer, Buff.)

The length of this bird is about seven inches and a half. The bill is brown; irides hazel; the general colour resembles that of a Lark; the throat white, the upper parts olive brown, each feather streaked down the middle with black; the under parts are dirty yellowish white, streaked on the sides with dark brown, and spotted with the same on the breast; the quills dusky, with yellowish edges; upper coverts tipped with white; tail feathers much the same as the wings, and somewhat forked: legs pale brown.

The Bunting is very common in all parts of the country, and may be frequently observed on the highest part of a hedge, or uppermost branch of a tree, uttering its harsh and dissonant cry, at short intervals; they are heard and seen in these situations during the greater part of summer, after which they are met with in flocks, and continue so during winter: they are often shot in great numbers, or caught in nets; and from the similarity of their plumage, are not infrequently sold for Larks. The female makes her nest among the thick grass, a little elevated above the ground; she lays five or six eggs. Buffon observes, that in France the Bunting is seldom seen during winter, but that it arrives soon after the Swallow, and spreads itself through almost every part of Europe. Their food consists chiefly of grain; they likewise eat the various kinds of insects which they find in the fields and meadows.

THE YELLOW BUNTING

Yellow Hammer, or Yellow Yowley

(Emberiza Citrinella, Linn.—*Le Bruant,* Buff.*)*

Length somewhat above six inches. Bill dusky; eyes hazel; the prevailing colour is yellow, mixed with brown of various shades; the crown of the head in general, is bright yellow, more or less variegated with brown; the cheeks, throat, and lower part of the belly pure yellow; the breast reddish, and the sides dashed with streaks of the same; the hinder part of the neck and back are greenish olive; the greater quills dusky, edged with pale yellow; lesser quills and scapulars dark brown, edged with grey; the tail is dusky, and a little forked, the feathers edged with light brown, the outermost with white; the legs yellowish brown. It is somewhat difficult to describe a species of bird of which no two are to be found perfectly similar, but its specific characters are plain, and cannot easily be mistaken. The colours of the female are less bright than those of the male, with very little yellow about the head.

This bird is common in every lane and hedge, flitting before the traveller as he passes along, or uttering its simple and frequently repeated monotone. It feeds on various kinds of seeds, insects, &c. The female makes an artless nest, composed of hay, dried roots, and moss, lined with hair and wool: she lays four or five eggs, marked with dark irregular streaks, and frequently has more than one brood in the season. In Italy, where small birds of almost every description are made use of for the table, this is esteemed very good eating, and is frequently fattened for that purpose like the Ortolan; but with us, who are accustomed to grosser kinds of food, it is considered too insignificant to form any part of our repasts.

THE CIRL BUNTING

(Emberiza Cirlus, Linn.—Le Bruant de haie ou Zizi, Buff.)

Length above six inches. Bill brown; the chin and throat dull black; upper part of the head and hinder part of the neck olive green; each feather streaked to the tip with dusky lines; the sides of the neck and breast yellowish green; the eyes are bedded in a dusky line; a yellow streak passes from above and beneath them; the auriculars the same colour; from behind these a yellow gorget falls down over the fore part of the neck to the breast; back and scapulars reddish bay, which is spread over each side of the lower part of the breast; the feathers of the first are slightly streaked and tipped with dusky, and all edged with a lighter shade; the lesser coverts are ash grey; the greater partake of that colour, but are tinged on the outer webs with pale brown, and on the inner with dusky; the quills and tail dusky, with pale edges; the two outside feathers of the latter are the longest, and their inner webs have each a stripe of white from a part of their shafts to their tips; the belly is yellow, with some dusky stripes towards the sides; the legs are tinged with pale reddish brown.

Latham says that these birds are found only in the warmer parts of France and Italy, but Montagu made them out to be British birds. Our figure is from a well-preserved specimen presented to the Newcastle Museum, by Mr Henry Mewburn, of St German's, Cornwall, where it was shot in 1822. This gentleman has besides ascertained that they breed in that neighbourhood, frequenting woods and high trees, and like the Common Bunting, generally perching near the top. They lay four or five greyish eggs, spotted and streaked with black.

THE BLACK-HEADED BUNTING

Reed Bunting, or Reed Sparrow

(Emberiza Schœniclus, Linn.—*L'Ortolan de Roseaux,* Buff.*)*

This is smaller than the Yellow Bunting. The eyes are hazel; the head, throat, fore part of the neck, and breast are black, excepting a white line from the corners of the bill, passing downward and forming a border reaching the back of the neck; the upper parts of the body and the wings are reddish brown, with a black streak down the centre of each feather; the under part of the body is white, with brown streaks on the sides; rump and upper tail coverts bluish ash, mixed with brown; quills dusky, edged with brown; the two middle feathers of the tail are black, edged pale brown; the rest wholly black, except the two outer ones, which are almost white, the ends tipped with brown, and the bases black; the legs and feet dusky brown. The female has no collar; her throat is not so black, and her head is variegated with black and rust colour; the white on her under parts is not so pure, but of a reddish cast.

Birds of this species frequent fens and marshy places, where there is abundance of rushes, among which they nestle. The nest is composed of dry grass, lined with the soft down of the reed; it is fixed with great art between four reed stalks, two on each side, almost close to each other, and about three feet above the water. The female lays four or five eggs, pale bluish white, veined irregularly with purple, principally at the larger end. As its chief resort is among reeds, it is supposed that the seeds of that plant are its principal food; it is however frequently seen in the higher grounds near the roads, and sometimes in cornfields. The male, during the time of hatching, has a soft, melodious, warbling song, whilst he sits perched among the reeds, and is frequently heard in the night-time. It is a timorous bird, very easily alarmed; in captivity it sings but little, and only when perfectly undisturbed.

THE TAWNY BUNTING

Great Pied Mountain Finch, or Brambling

(Emberiza mustelina, Gm. Linn.)

Length somewhat above six inches. Bill short, yellow, and blackish at the point; crown of the head tawny; forehead chestnut; hinder part of the neck and cheeks the same, but paler; throat, sides of the neck, and space round the eyes dirty white; breast dull yellow; under parts white, in some tinged with yellow; the back and scapulars black, edged with reddish brown; quill feathers dusky, edged with white; secondaries white on the outer edges; greater coverts tipped with white, which, when the wing is closed, forms a bed upon it; upper tail coverts yellow; tail a little forked, the two outermost feathers white, the third black, tipped with white, the rest wholly black; legs short and black; hinder claws almost as long, but more bent than those of the Lark. The foregoing figure and description were taken from a bird which was caught in the high moory grounds above Shotley-Kirk, Northumberland.

THE SPARROW

(Fringilla domestica, Linn.—*Le Moineau,* Buff.*)*

The length of this bird is five inches and three quarters: bill dusky, eyes hazel; the top of the head and back part of the neck ash grey; the throat, fore part of the neck, and space round the eyes black; the cheeks whitish; the breast and all the under parts pale ash; the back, scapulars, and wing coverts are reddish brown, mixed with black – the latter tipped with white, forming a light bar across the wing; the quills are dusky, with reddish edges; tail brown, edged with grey, and a little forked; legs pale brown. The female is distinguished from the male by wanting the black patch on the throat, and by having a little streak behind each eye; her whole plumage is also much plainer and duller.

This bird, as seen in large smoky towns, is generally dirty and unpleasing in its appearance; but among barns and stackyards the cock bird exhibits a very great variety in his plumage, and is far from being the least beautiful of our British birds.

The Sparrow never leaves us, but is familiar to the eye at all times, even in the most crowded and busy parts of a town: they build under the eaves of houses, in holes of walls, and often about churches. The nest is made of hay, carelessly put together, and lined with feathers. The female lays five or six eggs, of a reddish white, spotted with brown; she has generally three broods in the year, whence the multiplication of the species must be great. In autumn large flocks of them are seen everywhere, both in town and country. Though familiar, the Sparrow is a crafty bird, easily distinguishing the snares laid to entrap it; they often mix with other birds, and not infrequently partake with the Pigeons or the poultry, in spite of every precaution to prevent them.

THE GOLDFINCH

Goldspink, or Thistle-finch

(Fringilla Carduelis, Linn.—*Le Chardonneret,* Buff.*)*

The bill is white, tipped with black; the forehead and chin a rich scarlet, which is divided by a black line passing from each corner of the bill to the eyes, which are dark; the cheeks are white; top of the head black, which colour extends downward from the nape on each side, dividing the white on the cheeks from the white spot on the hinder part of the neck; the back and rump are cinnamon brown; the sides the same, but paler; belly white; lesser wing coverts black; quills black, marked in the middle of each feather with yellow, forming, when the wing is closed, a large patch; the tips white; the tail feathers are black, with a white spot on each near the end; legs pale flesh red.

Beauty of the plumage, says the lively Count de Buffon, melody of song, sagacity, and docility of disposition, seem all united in this charming little bird, which, were it rare, and imported from a foreign country, would be more highly valued. Goldfinches begin to sing early in the spring, and continue till the time of breeding is over; when kept in a cage, they will sing the greater part of the year. In a state of confinement they are much attached to their keepers, and will learn a variety of little tricks, such as to draw up small buckets containing their water and food, to fire a cracker, and such like. They construct a neat and compact nest, which is composed of moss, dried grass, and roots, lined with wool, hair, the down of thistles, and other soft and delicate substances. The female lays five white eggs, marked at the larger end with spots of deep purple. They feed their young with caterpillars and insects; the old birds feed on various kinds of seeds, particularly those of the thistle, and occasionally on the seeds of the Scotch fir.

THE SISKIN

Aberdevine

(Fringilla Spinus, Linn.—*Le Tarin,* Buff.*)*

Length nearly five inches. Bill white; eyes black; top of the head and throat black; over each eye there is a pale yellow streak; back of the neck and the back yellowish olive, marked with narrow dusky streaks down the middle of each feather; rump yellow; under parts greenish yellow, palest on the breast; thighs grey, marked with dusky streaks; greater wing coverts pale yellowish green, tipped with black; quills dusky, faintly edged with yellow, the outer web of each at the base fine pale yellow, forming, when the wing is closed, an irregular bar across it; the tail is forked, the middle feathers black, with faint edges, the outer ones yellow, with black tips: legs pale brown; claws white.

The foregoing figure and description were taken from one which was caught on the banks of the Tyne, and kept some years afterwards in a cage; its song, though not so loud as that of the Canary, was pleasing and sweetly various; it imitated the notes of other birds, even to the chirping of the Sparrow: it was familiar, docile, and cheerful, and began its song early in the morning. Like the Goldfinch, the Siskin may easily be taught to draw up its little bucket with water and food. The latter consists chiefly of seeds; it drinks frequently, and seems fond of throwing water over its feathers. It breeds freely with the Canary. When the Siskin is paired with the hen Canary, he is assiduous in his attention to his mate, carrying materials for the nest, and arranging them; and, during the time of incubation, regularly supplying the female with food.

THE GREATER REDPOLE
Greater Red-headed Linnet
(Fringilla cannabina, Linn.—La grande Linotte des Vignes, Buff.)

The length is five and a half inches; breadth nine and three quarters. The bill is thick at the base; the upper mandible dusky, the under one whitish. A pale brownish streak passes from the bill over and below each eye; the irides are dark; on the crown of the head is a bright crimson or lake-red spot; the rest of the head is ash grey, striped with brown on the back part, and mottled with the same colours on the brow, and on each side of the crown; the chin is yellowish; the hinder part and sides of the neck are dingy ash; the fore part dull white, spotted with dark brown. The breast[1] is of the same brilliant red as the crown of the head; the sides are pale reddish brown, fading into a dull white in the middle of the belly from the breast to the vent; the back, scapulars, and coverts of the wings are bright reddish brown, the middle of the feathers somewhat darker than the rest of the webs; the first quill feather is black, the eight next to it are the same, but white half their length on both the exterior and interior edges, the latter of which form a stripe of that colour when the wing

is closed. The tail is forked; the two middle feathers are narrow and pointed towards the tip, and wholly black; the rest are also black, but edged with white on both the outer and inner edges: the legs are dull brown. The female is without the red on her head and breast; in other respects her plumage is nearly the same as that of the male, but much less brilliant. In a wild state this charming bird wastes the sweetness of its song on the fells or heathy wastes which it almost constantly inhabits. There they build and rear their young, concealed in the prickly close branches of the whin. The nest is composed of the stems of dry grass, mixed with a little moss, and lined with horse hair. The female commonly lays five eggs; they are white, with a zone of freckles and small brown spots near the thicker end.

1 *It loses the red breast in the autumn, and assumes it again in the spring; in this it differs from the Grey Linnet, whose plumage continues the same in all seasons.* [Bewick's note]

THE LESSER REDPOLE

(Fringilla Linaria, Linn.—*Le Sizerin*, Buff.*)*

Length about five inches. Bill pale brown, point dusky; eyes hazel; the forehead is marked with a large pretty spot, of a deep red inclining to purple; the breast is of the same colour, but less bright; the feathers on the back are dusky, edged with pale brown; the greater and lesser coverts tipped with dirty white, forming two light bars across the wing; the belly and thighs dull white; the quills and tail dusky, edged with dirty white; the latter somewhat forked: legs dusky. In our bird the rump was reddish. The female has no red on the breast or rump, and the spot on her forehead is of a saffron colour; her plumage in general is not so bright as that of the male.

This species is found in every part of Europe. In America and the northern parts of Asia it is likewise very common. They are not infrequent in this island; they breed chiefly in the northern parts, and are known by the name of French Linnets. They make a shallow open nest, composed of dried grass and wool, lined with hair and feathers: the female lays four eggs, almost white, marked with reddish spots. In winter they mix with other birds, and migrate in flocks to the southern counties; they feed on small seeds of various kinds, especially those of the alder, of which they are extremely fond; they hang like the Titmouse, with their back downwards, upon the branches, while feeding, and in this situation may easily be caught with lime twigs.

THE LINNET
Brown or Grey Linnet
(*Fringilla Linota*, Linn.—*La Linotte*, Buff.)

ength about five inches and a half. The bill bluish grey; eyes hazel; upper parts of the head, the neck, and back, dark reddish brown, edges of the feathers pale; under parts dirty reddish white; breast deeper than the rest, sides streaked with brown; quills dusky, edged with white; tail brown, likewise with white edges, except the two middle feathers, which have reddish margins; it is somewhat forked: legs short and brown. The female is marked on the breast with streaks of brown; she has less white on her wings, and her colours in general are less bright.

This bird is very well known, being common in every part of Europe; and is met with chiefly on moory grounds: it builds its nest concealed in furze bushes; the outside is made up of dry grass, roots, and moss; it is lined with hair and wool. The female lays four or five eggs, they are white, tinged with blue, and irregularly spotted with brown at the larger end: she breeds generally twice in the year. The song of the Linnet is lively and sweetly varied; its manners are gentle, and its disposition docile; it easily adopts the song of other birds, when confined with them, and in some instances it has been taught to pronounce words with great distinctness; but this substitution of imperfect and forced accents, which have neither charms nor beauty, in the room of the free and varied modulations of uninstructed nature, is a perversion of its talents. Linnets are frequently found in flocks: during winter, they feed on various seeds, and are particularly fond of lintseed, from which circumstance, it is said, they derive their name.

THE PIED FLYCATCHER

Coldfinch

(Muscicapa Atricapilla, Linn.—Le Traquet d'Angleterre, Buff.)

Length nearly five inches. Bill black; eyes hazel; forehead white; top of the head, the back, and the tail black; the rump is dashed with ash; wing coverts dusky, greater coverts tipped with white; the exterior sides of the secondary quills are white, as are also the outer feathers of the tail; all the under parts, from the bill to the tail, are white; legs black. The female is much smaller, but longer tailed than the male; she is brown where he is black; she likewise wants the white spot on the forehead.

This bird is nowhere common; it is said to be most plentiful in Yorkshire, Lancashire, and Derbyshire. Since the cut was finished, which was done from a drawing presented to the Editor, we have been favoured with a pair of these birds, shot at Benton, in Northumberland: we suppose them to be male and female, as one of them wanted the white spot on the forehead; in other respects it was similar to the male: the upper parts in both were black, obscurely mixed with brown; the quill feathers dark reddish brown; tail dark brown, the exterior edge of the outer feather white; legs black.

The nest of this bird, with a very great number of young, was found in a hole of a tree, in Axwell Park, June 18, 1801: the parent birds, but particularly the male, were extremely expert in catching the small flies with which they incessantly fed their young. The female, after she had fed her young, always jerked up her tail.

THE SPOTTED FLYCATCHER

Beam Bird

(*Muscicapa Grisola*, Linn.—*Le Gobe mouche*, Buff.)

Length nearly five inches and three quarters: bill broad, flatted, and wide at the base, where it is beset with a few short bristles; a ridge runs along the upper mandible; that and the under one are dusky at the tips, the latter is yellowish towards the base; inside of the mouth yellow: all the upper plumage is of a mouse colour, darkest on the wings and tail: head and neck more or less obscurely spotted with dark brown; the wing coverts, secondary quills, and scapulars, also dark brown, edged with dingy white; under parts very pale ash, or lint-coloured white, tinged with rufous on the sides and breast, which latter is marked with streaks of brown: the legs are short, and darkish.

The Flycatcher, of all our summer birds, is the most mute. It visits this island in the spring, and disappears in September. The female builds her nest commonly in gardens, on any projecting stone in a wall, or on the end of a beam, screened by the leaves of a vine, sweet-briar, or woodbine, and sometimes close to the post of a door, where people are going in and out all day long. The nest is rather carelessly made; it is composed chiefly of moss and dried grass, mixed in the inside with some wool, and a few hairs. She lays four or five eggs, of a dull white, closely spotted and blotched with rusty red. This bird feeds on insects, for which it sits watching on a branch or on a post, suddenly dropping down upon them, and catching them on the wing, and immediately rising, returns again to its station to wait for more. After the young have quitted the nest, the parent birds follow them from tree to tree, and watch them with the most sedulous attention. They feed them with the flies which flutter among the boughs beneath; or pursuing their insect prey with a quick irregular kind of flight, like that of a butterfly, to a greater distance, they immediately return as before described.

THE LARK
Skylark or Lavrock
(Alauda arvensis, Linn.—L'Alouette, Buff.)

Length nearly seven inches. Bill dusky, under mandible somewhat yellow; eyes hazel; over each eye a pale streak, which extends to the bill, and round the eye on the under side; on the upper parts of the body the feathers are of a reddish brown colour, dark in the middle, with pale edges; the fore part of the neck is reddish white, spotted with brown; breast, belly, and thighs white; the quills brown, with pale edges; tail the same, and somewhat forked, the two middle feathers darkest, the outermost white on the outer edge; the legs dusky. In some of our specimens the feathers on the top of the head were long, and formed a sort of crest behind.

The Lark begins its song very early in spring, and is heard chiefly in the morning. Shakespeare thus beautifully describes its rising:

Lo! hear the gentle Lark, weary of rest

From his moist cabinet mounts up on high,
And wakes the morning, from whose silver breast
The sun ariseth in his majesty.

It rises in the air almost perpendicularly and by successive springs, and hovers at a vast height; its descent, on the contrary, is in an oblique direction, unless it is threatened by birds of prey, or attracted by its mate, and on these occasions it drops like a stone. It makes its nest on the ground, between two clods of earth, and lines it with dried grass and roots: the female lays four or five eggs, of a greyish brown, marked with darker spots; she generally has two broods in the year, and sits only about fifteen days. As soon as the young have escaped from the nest, the attachment of the parent seems to increase; she flutters over their heads, directs all their motions, and is ever ready to screen them from danger.

THE FIELD LARK
Rock Lark
(Alauda campestris, Linn.—La Spipolette, Buff.)

This bird is six inches and seven eighths in length, and eleven inches and three eighths in breadth. The bill is rather slender; irides hazel; a pale streak extends from the upper part of the beak over the eyes, and a dark one underneath; the plumage on the head, neck, back, wings, tertials, and tail, looks altogether of a deep olive brown, but on a nearer inspection, each feather is dark in the middle, and lighter towards the edges; but the lower part of the back is not clouded, being more uniformly pale olive, or greenish brown; the two outside feathers of the tail are brownish white the whole length of their outer margins, and the inner web is the same, about halfway from the end. In our figure, which was taken from a stuffed specimen, the tertial feathers were nearly the length of the quills, which latter are narrowly edged on the outer webs with pale greenish brown; the under parts, from the throat to the vent, are of a pale dingy yellow, spotted on the fore part of the neck, and clouded or striped on the breast and sides with olive brown. The legs are pale brownish red; the hind claws long and curved. This bird is mostly met with among the rocks on the promontories and isles near the sea shore: it builds its nest, commonly, in the crevices near the tops of those where the earth has crumbled down and made a lodgment; it is rather large, and is wholly composed of the small blades and stems of dried grass. The eggs, five in number, are closely freckled with ash, and sprinkled with small brown spots.

84

THE TREE LARK

Lesser Field Lark

(Alauda minor, Gm. Linn.*)*

This bird measures six inches and three eighths in length, and ten inches in breadth. The upper mandible is dusky; the under one pale, with a blush of red: the upper part of the head, and hinder part of the neck are dingy light brown, streaked with very dark brown spots; the back feathers are more olive, also streaked with dark brown; the lower part of the back, the rump, and upper tail coverts are dull olive brown, lightest on the edges; the tail feathers are deep brown, with lighter edges; the two outside ones dull white on the margins and tips; the two next to them tipped with a spot of white; the chin, throat, and fore part of the neck and breast are dull yellow, the latter spotted very dark brown; the belly and vent dingy white: sides reddish yellow, with narrow brown streaks: the ridge of the wings, and part of the lesser coverts are olive brown; the feathers next the greater coverts dark brown, deeply edged with dull white; all the rest of the wing feathers are darkish brown, more or less margined with pale edges: legs and toes dull yellow.

This bird frequents woods and plantations, and sits on the highest tree branches, whence it rises singing, to a considerable height, and descends slowly, with wings set up and tail spread out like a fan. Its note is full, clear, and melodious. It nests on the ground, commonly at the root of a bush, near the edge of a coppice or plantation. The outside is made of moss; the inside of the stems of dried grass. The seven eggs are blotched with deep vinous purple; the ground colour partakes of a tint of the same, but much paler.

85

THE TITLARK

(Alauda pratensis, Linn.—La Farlouse, ou L'Alouette de prez, Buff.)

Is five inches and a half in length. The bill is black at the tip, and yellowish brown at the base; the eyes hazel, and over each is a pale streak. In the disposition of the colours it is very similar to the Skylark, but somewhat darker on the upper parts, and inclining to a greenish brown. The breast is beautifully spotted with black on a light yellowish ground; the belly light ash, obscurely streaked on the sides with dusky; the tail is almost black, the two outer feathers white on the exterior edges, the outermost but one tipped with a white spot on the end: the legs are yellowish; feet and claws brown. The plumage of the female is less bright than that of the male.

The Titlark is common in this country; and, though it sometimes perches on trees, is generally found in meadows and low marshy grounds. It makes its nest of withered grass, commonly on the ground, but sometimes on the side of a brae: the nest is like that of the Rock Lark, but the eggs are different both in size and colour; the female lays five eggs, very closely freckled with deep brown: the young are hatched about the beginning of June. During the time of incubation, the male sits on a neighbouring tree, rising at times and singing. The Titlark is flushed with the least noise, and shoots with a rapid flight. Its note is fine, but short, and without much variety; it warbles in the air in humble imitation of the Skylark, and increases its song as it descends slowly to the branch on which it chooses to perch. It is further distinguished by the shake of its tail, particularly whilst it eats.

THE WOODLARK

(Alauda arborea, Linn.—*L'Alouette de bois*, Buff.*)*

This bird is somewhat smaller than the Field Lark: the colours of its plumage are much the same, but on the upper parts paler, and not so distinctly defined: a white streak passes from the bill over each eye nearly to the nape; the under parts are white, tinged with yellow on the throat, and red on the breast, and spotted with black. The tail is shorter than that of other Larks, which gives this bird a less tall and slender shape: the legs are dull yellow; the hinder claw very long, and somewhat curved.

The Woodlark is generally found near the borders of woods, from which it derives its name; it perches on trees, and sings during the night, so as sometimes to be mistaken for the Nightingale; it likewise sings as it flies, and builds its nest on the ground, similar to that of the Skylark. The female lays five eggs, of a dusky hue, marked with brown spots. It builds very early, the young, in some seasons, being able to fly about the latter end of March. It makes two nests in the year, like the Skylark, but is not nearly so numerous as that bird.

THE PIED WAGTAIL
Black and White Water Wagtail
(Motacilla alba, Linn.—*La Lavandière,* Buff.*)*

Length about seven inches. The bill is black; eyes hazel; hinder part of the head and neck black; forehead, cheeks, and sides of the neck white; the fore part of the neck and part of the breast are black, bordered by a line of white, in the form of a gorget; the back and rump are dark ash; wing coverts and secondary quills dusky, edged with light grey; prime quills black, with pale edges; lower part of the breast and belly white; the middle feathers of the tail are black, the outermost white, except at the base and tips of the inner webs, which are black: legs black. There are slight variations in these birds; some are white on the chin and throat, leaving only a crescent of black on the breast. The head of the female is brown.

This is a very common bird with us, and may be seen everywhere, running on the ground, and leaping after flies and other insects, on which it feeds. Its usual haunts are the shallow margins of springs and running waters, into which it will sometimes wade a little in pursuit of its food. They make their nest on the ground, of dry grass, moss, and small roots, lined with hair and feathers, and have been known sometimes to breed in the deserted nest of the Swallow, in chimneys; the female lays five white eggs, spotted with brown. They are very attentive to their young, and continue to feed and train them for three or four weeks after they are able to fly: they defend them with great courage when in danger, or endeavour to draw aside the enemy by various little arts. They are very attentive to the cleanliness of the nest, and have been known to remove light substances, such as paper or straw, which have been laid as a mark to find it by.

The Wagtail is said by some authors to migrate into other climates about the end of October; with us it is known to change its quarters as the winter approaches, from north to south. Its note is small and insignificant but frequently repeated, especially while on the wing.

THE GREY WAGTAIL

(Motacilla Boarula, Linn.—La Bergeronette jaune, Buff.)

Is somewhat longer than the last. Bill dark brown; over each eye a pale streak; head, neck, and back ash grey; throat and chin black; rump and under part bright yellow; wing coverts and quills dark brown, the former with pale edges; tertials, almost as long as the greater quills, white at the base, and edged with yellow on the outer webs; middle tail feathers black, outer ones white: legs yellowish brown.

The habits of this bird are similar to those of the last. It builds on the ground, and sometimes on the banks of rivulets, laying six or eight eggs, of a dirty white, with yellow spots. The female has no black on the throat.

THE YELLOW WAGTAIL

(Motacilla flava, Linn.—La Bergeronette de printemps, Buff.)

Length six inches and a half. Bill black; eyes hazel; the head and all the upper parts of the body are olive green, palest on the rump; the under parts bright yellow, dashed with a few dull spots on the breast and belly; over each eye is a pale yellow streak, and beneath a dusky line, curving upwards towards the hinder part of the head; wing coverts edged with pale yellow; quills dusky; tail black, except the outer feathers, which are white: legs black; hinder claws long.

This bird is seen very early in the spring, in the meadows and fields, among the green corn, where it frequently nestles; in winter it haunts the sides of brooks and springs which do not freeze. The female lays five eggs, of a pale lead colour, with dusky spots.

THE NIGHTINGALE

(Motacilla Luscinia, Linn.—La Rossignol, Buff.)

This bird, so universally esteemed for the excellence of its song, is not remarkable for the variety or richness of its plumage. It is somewhat more than six inches in length. The bill brown, yellow on the edges at the base; eyes hazel; the whole upper part of the body rusty brown, tinged with olive; the under parts pale ash, almost white at the throat and vent; the quills brown, with reddish margins: legs pale brown. The male and female are very similar.

Although the Nightingale is common in this country, it never visits the northern parts of our island, and is but seldom seen in the western counties of Devonshire and Cornwall: it leaves us sometime in the month of August, and makes its regular return in the beginning of April; it is supposed, during that interval, to visit the distant regions of Asia; this is probable, as these birds do not winter in any part of France, Germany, Italy, Greece, &c. neither does it appear that they stay in Africa, but are seen at all times in India, Persia, China, and Japan; in the latter country they are much esteemed for their song, and sell at great prices. They are spread generally throughout Europe, even as far north as Siberia and Sweden, where they are said to sing delightfully; they, however, are partial to particular places, and avoid others which seem as likely to afford them the necessary means of support. It is not improbable, however, that by planting a colony in a well-chosen situation, these charming songsters might be induced to haunt places where they are not at present seen; the experiment might be easily tried, and should it succeed, the reward would be great in the rich and varied song of this unrivalled bird. Milton gives us the following beautiful description:—

And the mute silence hist along,
'Less Philomel will deign a song,
In her sweetest, saddest plight,
Smoothing the rugged brow of night,
While Cynthia checks her dragon yoke,
Gently o'er the accustomed oak:
Sweet bird that shunn'st the noise of folly,
Most musical, most melancholy!
Thee, chauntress, oft the woods among,
I woo to hear thy evening song:

Nightingales begin to build about the end of April or the beginning of May; they make their nest in the lower part of a thick bush or hedge; the female lays four or five eggs of a greenish brown colour. The nest is composed of dry grass and leaves, intermixed with small fibres, and lined with hair, down, and other soft and warm substances. The business of incubation is entirely performed by the female, whilst the male, at no great distance, entertains her with his delightful melody: as soon, however, as the young are hatched, he leaves off singing, and joins her in the care of providing for them. These birds make a second hatch, and sometimes a third; and in hot countries they are said to have four.

The Nightingale is a solitary bird, and never unites in flocks like many of the smaller birds, but hides itself in the thickest parts of the bushes, and sings generally in the night: its food consists principally of insects, small worms, eggs of ants, and sometimes berries of various kinds. Though timorous and shy, they are easily caught; lime twigs and snares of all sorts are laid for them, and generally succeed. Young ones are sometimes brought up from the nest, and fed with great care till they are able to sing. It is with great difficulty that old birds are induced to sing after being taken; for a considerable time they refuse to eat, but by great attention to their treatment, and avoiding everything that might agitate them, they at length resume their song, and continue it during the greater part of the year.

THE DARTFORD WARBLER

(Motacilla provincialis, Linn.*—Le Pitchou de Provence,* Buff.*)*

This bird measures above five inches in length, of which the tail is about one half. The bill is rather long and slender, and a little bent at the tip; it is black, and whitish at the base; the eyes are reddish; eyelids deep crimson; all the upper parts dark rusty brown, tinged with dull yellow; the breast, part of the belly, and thighs deep red, inclining to rust colour; the middle of the belly white; the bastard wing is also white; tail dusky, except the exterior web of the outer feather, which is white: legs yellow.

It seems to be a rare bird in this country, and owes its name, with us, to the accident of a pair of them having been seen near Dartford, in Kent, some years ago; they have since been observed in great numbers, and are supposed sometimes to winter with us. Our figure was from a specimen now in the Newcastle Museum.

THE REDBREAST

Robin-redbreast, or Ruddock

(Motacilla rubecula, Linn.—*Le Rouge Gorge,* Buff.*)*

This general favourite is too well known to need a very minute description. The bill is slender and delicate; its eyes large, black, and expressive, and its aspect mild; the head and all the upper parts are brown, tinged with greenish olive; neck and breast of a fine deep reddish orange; a spot of the same colour marks its forehead; belly and vent dull white: legs dusky.

In spring the Redbreast retires to woods and thickets, where, with its mate, it prepares for the accommodation of its future family. During summer it is rarely to be seen. The nest is placed near the ground, by the roots of trees, in the most concealed spot, and sometimes in old buildings, and is constructed of moss and dried leaves, intermixed with hair, and lined with feathers: in order more effectually to conceal it, they cover it over with leaves,

leaving only a narrow winding entrance under the heap. The female lays from five to nine eggs, of a dull white, marked with reddish spots. During the time of incubation, the male sits at no great distance, and makes the woods resound with his delightful warble; he keenly chases all the birds of his own species, and drives them from his little settlement; for it has never been known that two pairs of these birds, who are as faithful as they are amorous, were lodged at the same time in the same bush. The Redbreast prefers the thick shade, where there is water; it feeds on insects and worms; but never eats them alive. It takes them in its bill and beats them against the ground till they cease to move: during this operation it frequently happens that the caterpillar is burst, and its entrails are shaken out, leaving only the body thus cleansed from all its impurities. Some ornithologists have ascribed this to the extreme delicacy of the bird in preparing its repast; others think that it is only an accidental consequence arising from the manner of putting its prey to death.

Although the Redbreast never quits this island, it performs a partial migration. As soon as the business of incubation is over, and the young are sufficiently grown to provide for themselves, he leaves his retirement,[1] and again draws near the habitations of mankind: his well-known familiarity has attracted the attention and secured the protection of man in all ages; he haunts the dwelling of the cottager, and partakes of his humble fare: when the cold grows severe, and snow covers the ground, he approaches the house, taps at the window with his bill, as if to entreat an asylum, which is always cheerfully granted, and with a simplicity the most delightful, hops round the house, picks up crumbs, and seems to make himself one of the family. Thomson has described the annual visits of this little guest, in the following lines:—

The Redbreast, sacred to the household gods,
Wisely regardful of th' embroiling sky,
In joyless fields and thorny thickets leaves
His shivering mates, and pays to trusted man
His annual visit. Half afraid, he first
Against the window beats; then brisk alights
On the warm hearth; then, hopping o'er the floor,

Eyes all the smiling family askance,
And pecks, and starts, and wonders where he is;
Till, more familiar grown, the table crumbs
Attract his slender feet.

The young Redbreast, when full feathered, may be taken for a different bird, being all over besprinkled with rust-coloured spots on a light ground: the first appearance of the red is about the end of August, but it does not attain its full colour till the end of the following month. Redbreasts are never seen in flocks, but always singly; and, when all other birds associate together, they still retain their solitary habits. Buffon says, that as soon as the young birds have attained their full plumage, they prepare for their departure; but in thus changing their situation, they do not gather in flocks, but perform their journey singly, one after another, which is a singular circumstance in the history of this bird. Its general familiarity has occasioned it to be distinguished by a peculiar name in many countries: about Bornholm, it is called Tomi Liden; in Norway, Peter Ronsmad; in Germany, it is called Thomas Gierdet; and with us, Robin-Redbreast, or Ruddock.

1 *The Redbreast, as well as some other kinds of birds, visits the seashores in the autumn. [Bewick's note]*

THE REDSTART

(Motacilla Phoenicurus, Linn.—*Le Rossignol de Muraille,* Buff.*)*

Measures rather more than five inches in length. The bill and eyes are black; forehead white; cheeks, throat, fore part and sides of the neck black, which colour extends over each eye; the crown of the head, hinder part of the neck, and the back are of a deep blue grey; in some, probably old birds, this grey is almost black; the breast, rump, and sides are of a fine glowing red, inclining to orange, which extends to all the feathers of the tail, excepting the two middle ones, which are brown; the belly is white; feet and claws black. The female differs considerably from the male; her colours are not so vivid: the top of the head and back are ash grey; chin white.

The Redstart is migratory; it appears about the middle of April, and departs in the end of September, or beginning of October; it frequents old walls and ruinous edifices, where it makes its nest, composed chiefly of moss, lined with hair and feathers. It is distinguished by a peculiar quick shake of its tail from side to side, when it alights. Though wild and timorous, it is frequently found in the midst of cities, always choosing the most inaccessible places for its residence: it likewise builds in forests, in holes of trees, or in high and dangerous precipices. The female lays four or five eggs, not much unlike those of the Hedge-warbler, but somewhat longer. These birds feed on flies, spiders, the eggs of ants, small berries, soft fruits, and suchlike. The young are thickly freckled with tawny spots, and might readily be mistaken for the young of the Redbreast, but for the vivid horizontal motion of the tail, which begins as soon as they fly.

THE REED WARBLER

Sedge Bird, or Reed Wren

(Motacilla Salicaria, Linn.—La Fauvette de roseaux, Buff.)

Length five inches. Bill dusky; eyes hazel; crown of the head and back brown, with dusky streaks; rump tawny; cheeks brown; over each eye a light streak; wing coverts dusky, edged with pale brown, as are the quills and tail; throat, breast, and belly are white, the latter tinged with yellow; thighs yellow; legs dusky; the hinder claws much bent.

It frequents the sides of rivers and ponds, and also places where reeds and sedges grow, and builds there; the nest is made of dried grass, and tender fibres of plants, lined with hair, and usually contains five eggs of a dirty white, mottled with brown: it sings night and day, during the breeding time, imitating by turns the notes of various birds, from which it is also called the English Mock bird. The whole of this genus are so shy, that they will quit the nest if it be touched by anyone.

THE GRASSHOPPER WARBLER

Grasshopper Lark,—Pennant.

(Sylvia Locustella, Lath.—Fauvette Tachetée, Buff.)

This bird is between five and six inches in length, and of a slender form. The tail is cuneiform and rather long, as well as the legs; the wings short, reaching very little beyond the base of the tail. The irides are hazel; upper mandible dusky, the under one yellowish white towards the base: a brown streak passes from the bill to the eye, and a white one above it; the crown of the head, hinder part of the neck, shoulders, and upper part of the back are brown, with a slight tinge of olive, the middle of each feather dusky; the wings are nearly of the same colour, the feathers being dark in the middle, edged with pale brown; the lower part of the back, upper tail coverts, and tail are pale brown; the throat and fore part of the neck are yellowish white, with a few darkish spots on the upper part of the breast; the sides of the neck, and all the under parts are pale dingy yellow; legs nearly the same.

This bird is seldom seen, and is best known by the lengthened grinding, sibilous noise which it makes about the dusk of a still summer's evening. It artfully skulks among old furze bushes, or in the thickest brakes and hedges, from which it will not easily be forced away. We were favoured with the drawing from which our figure is taken, by Mr R. R. Wingate, and also with a sight of its nest which is composed of coarse dried grass, and about three inches in thickness, but very shallow; it contained five beautiful white eggs, closely freckled with carnation spots. Mr W. gives the following account of the manner in which it places its nest. Having long wished to get the eggs, he, in June, 1815, succeeded in eyeing the bird to the distant passage on the top of a whin bush, by which it entered and left its nest. This he found was built at the bottom of a deep narrow furrow or ditch, overhung by the prickly branches of the whin, and grown over with thick coarse grass, matted together to the height of about two feet; all which he was obliged to take away piece-meal, before he succeeded in gaining the prize.

THE BLACK-CAP

(Motacilla Atricapilla, Linn.—*La Fauvette à tête noire*, Buff.*)*

Is somewhat above five inches in length. The upper mandible is of a dark horn colour; the under one light blue, and the edges of both whitish; top of the head black; sides of the head and hinder part of the neck ash colour; back and wings olive grey; the throat, breast, belly, and vent more or less silvery white; the legs bluish, inclining to brown; claws black. The head of the female is of a dull rust colour.

The Black-cap visits us about the middle of April, and retires in September; it frequents gardens, and builds its nest near the ground, commonly among the branches of the woodbine; it is very slightly made, and composed of the dried stems and curled roots of small grass, thinly interwoven with a very few hairs, and bound to the twigs with the cotton of plants; the inside of the nest is deep and round; the eggs, commonly five in number, are reddish brown, sprinkled or marbled with spots of a much darker colour. During the time of incubation the male sits by turns, he likewise procures the female food, such as flies, worms, and insects. The Black-cap sings sweetly, and so like the Nightingale, that in Norfolk it is called the Mock-Nightingale; it also imitates the Thrush and the Blackbird. Our ingenious countryman, White, observes, that it has usually a full, sweet, deep, loud, and wild pipe, yet the strain is of short continuance, and its motions desultory; but when this bird sits calmly, and in earnest engages in song, it pours forth very sweet but inward melody, and expresses great variety of sweet and gentle modulations, superior, perhaps, to any of our warblers, the Nightingale excepted; and, while it warbles, its throat is wonderfully distended. Black-caps feed chiefly on flies and insects, but not infrequently on ivy and other berries, and the seeds of the euonymus.

THE WHITETHROAT

(Motacilla Sylvia, Linn.—La Fauvette grise, Buff.)

Length about five inches and a half. Bill dark brown, lighter at the base; eyes dark hazel; the upper part of the head and back are reddish ash; throat white; lesser wing coverts pale brown; the greater dusky brown, with reddish margins; breast and belly silvery white; the wings and tail dusky brown, with pale edges, outer feathers white: legs pale brown. The breast and belly of the female are entirely white.

This bird arrives with the Redstart, Black-cap, &c. in the spring, and quits us in autumn about the same time that they do; it frequents thickets and hedges, and feeds on insects and wild berries. It builds in thick bushes, the nest is composed of fine dried grass, thinly lined with hair: the female lays five eggs, of a greenish white, sprinkled with darkish olive spots, which become numerous and blotched at the thicker end. It is often heard in the midst of a thick covert to utter a pretty constant grating call of cha, cha, cha, which it leaves off as soon as it is disturbed, flitting before the passenger from bush to bush, singing as it flies along, and sometimes mounting up a little height into the air, as if it were attempting to imitate the Lark, both in its motions and song; but in these it falls greatly short, and its frequently repeated notes have but little melody.

THE LESSER WHITETHROAT

(Motacilla Sylviella, Linn.)

This bird is of a slender shape, like the Willow Wren, and from its shy disposition, is not often seen. By those who have watched its motions, it is described as darting like a mouse through the interior branches of the brakes and underwoods, among which it shelters itself. Its length is four inches and seven eighths, breadth seven inches and a quarter, weight six drachms. The irides are dark hazel; both mandibles are dark at the tips; the under one yellowish towards the base. The upper plumage is of a mouse-coloured brown; the scapulars and quills nearly the same, edged with lighter brown; and the two outside feathers of the tail, with dull white: the under parts, from the chin to the vent, are more or less of a silvery white; legs, toes, and claws brown.

Our figure was taken from a bird which was shot in the boundary hedge of Newcastle Town Moor, on the 2nd June, 1815, and presented to this work by Mr R. R. Wingate. Its nest was built in a woodbine bush, about a yard from the ground: it was of a slight fabric, composed of the dried stems of small grass, and curled small roots, and very thinly interwoven or lined with a few hairs. The eggs, five in number, were white, spotted with brown, and intermixed with other spots of a pale bluish ash. They are somewhat less than those of the Whitethroat, and differently marked.

THE WILLOW WREN

(Le Figuier brun et jaune, Buff.)

This is next in size. The plumage of the upper parts is darker than that of the last, and of an olive green; the wings are brown, with dull yellow edges; under parts whitish, pretty deeply tinged with yellow on the throat, breast, and thighs: the bill is brown, inside yellow; over each eye a light yellow line extends from the bill to the back part of the head: the legs are yellow brown. These birds vary in the shadings of their plumage.

The Willow Wren frequents hedges and shrubberies; its food consists of insects, in search of which it is continually running up and down small branches of trees. Its nest is placed on the ground, commonly on the side or edge of a brae; it is composed of a great quantity of moss and dried grass, lined with long coarse hair and feathers: it lays six white eggs, beautifully spotted with red.

THE CHIFF CHAFF

Length nearly five inches; breadth seven and a quarter; weight about a quarter of an ounce; upper plumage dark olive green; the under partakes of a *blea* lint white, slightly tinged with yellow; a pale dull yellow line extends from the bill over the eyes towards the nape; bill dark with yellow edges; primaries, secondaries, and tail brown, edged with pale green; legs yellowish brown. They visit this country among the first summer birds of passage, but from their preferring shady woods, or tall trees, they are seldom to be seen.[1]

1 *Seven of these birds have recently been shot, some of them while in the act of calling 'chiff chaff,' and presented to this work, by Mr W. Proctor. They all exhibited nearly the same plumage. [Bewick's note]*

THE GOLDEN-CRESTED WREN

(Motacilla Regulus, Linn.—*Le Roitelet,* Buff.*)*

This is supposed to be the least of all European birds; it is certainly the smallest of the British kinds, being in length not quite three inches and a half,[1] and weighing only seventy-six grains. The bill is very slender and dark; eyes hazel; on the top of its head the feathers are of a bright orange colour, bordered on each side with black, which forms an arch above the eyes, and with which it sometimes conceals the crown, by contracting the muscles of the head: the upper part of the body is yellowish olive green; all the under parts pale reddish white, tinged with green on the sides; the greater coverts of the wings are dusky brown, edged with yellow, and tipped with white: quills dusky, edged with pale green, as are the tail feathers, but lighter: legs yellowish brown. The female is distinguished by a pale yellow crown: her whole plumage is less vivid than that of the male.

This most pleasing fairy bird delights in large trees, such as oaks, elms, tall pines, and firs, particularly the first, in which it finds both food and shelter; in these it builds its nest, suspended from a branch by a kind of cordage made of the materials of which the nest is chiefly composed; it is oblong, with an aperture on one side, and is made principally of moss, lined with the softest down: the female lays six or seven eggs, scarcely larger than peas, which are white, sprinkled with very small spots of a dull colour. These birds are very agile, and almost continually in motion, fluttering from branch to branch, creeping on all sides of the trees, and often hanging like the Titmouse. Their food consists chiefly of the smallest insects, which they find in the crevices of the bark of trees, or catch nimbly on the wing; they also eat the eggs of insects, small worms, and various sorts of seeds.

The Golden-crested Wren is diffused throughout Europe; it has also been met with in America and Asia. It stays with us the whole year, even so far north as the Orkney Islands. Its song is very melodious, but weaker than that of the Common Wren: it has besides a sharp shrill cry like that of a Grasshopper.

1 *The body, when stripped of its feathers, is about an inch long.*
   [Bewick's note]

THE WREN

Kitty Wren

(Motacilla Troglodytes, Linn.—*Le Troglodyte,* Buff.*)*

Length three inches and a half. The bill is slender, and a little curved; upper mandible and tips of a brownish horn colour, the under one, and edges of both, dull yellow; a whitish line extends from the bill over the eyes, which are dark hazel; the upper parts of the plumage are clear brown, marked on the back and rump with narrow double wavy lines of pale and dark brown; belly, sides, and thighs are marked the same, but more distinctly; the throat is dingy white; cheeks and breast the same, faintly dappled with brown; the quills and tail are marked with alternate bars of a reddish brown and black; legs pale olive brown.

This active little bird is very common in England, and braves our severest winters, which it contributes to enliven by its sprightly note. During that season it takes shelter in the roofs of houses, barns, and in haystacks; it sings till late in the evening, and not infrequently during a fall of snow. In the spring it betakes itself to the woods, where it builds on the ground, or in a low bush, and sometimes on the turf, beneath a tree trunk, or in a hole in a wall: its nest is oval-shaped, with one small aperture in the side: it is composed chiefly of moss, or other nearby materials, and lined within with feathers: the female lays from ten to eighteen eggs; they are white, thinly sprinkled with small reddish spots, mostly at the thicker end.

THE WHEATEAR
White-rump

(Motacilla Oenanthe, Linn.—*Le Moteux, ou le Culblanc,* Buff.*)*

Length five inches and a half. Bill black; eyes hazel; from the base of the bill a black streak is extended over the eyes, cheeks, and ears, where it is pretty broad; above this there is a line of white; the top of the head, hinder part of the neck, and the back, are bluish grey; the wing coverts and quills dusky, edged with rusty white; the rump is perfectly white, as is part of the tail; the rest black; the under parts are pale buff, tinged with red on the breast: legs and feet black. In the female the white line above the eye is somewhat obscure, and all the black parts of the plumage incline more to brown; neither is the tail of so pure a white.

The Wheatear breeds under shelter of a tuft or clod, in newly-ploughed lands, or under stones, and sometimes in old rabbit burrows: the nest is constructed with great care, of dry grass or moss, mixed with wool, lined with feathers, and defended by a sort of covert fixed to the stone or clod under which it is formed: the female generally lays five or six light blue eggs, the larger end encompassed with a circle of a somewhat deeper hue.

This bird visits us about the middle of March, and from that time till May is seen to arrive: it frequents new-tilled grounds, and never fails to follow the plough in search of insects and small worms, which are its principal food. In some parts of England great numbers are taken in snares made of horse hair, placed beneath a turf; near two thousand dozen are said to have been taken annually in that way, in one district only, and are generally sold at sixpence per dozen.[1] They leave us in August and September, and about that time are seen in great numbers by the seashore, where, probably, they subsist some little time before they take their departure. They are extended over a large portion of the globe, even as far as the southern parts of Asia.

1 *Pennant. [Bewick's note]*

THE WHINCHAT

(Motacilla Rubetra, Linn.—Le grand Traquet, ou le Tarier, Buff.)

This bird is somewhat larger than the Stonechat. The bill is black; eyes hazel; the feathers on the head, neck, and back are black, bordered with rust colour; a streak of white passes from the bill over each eye towards the hinder part of the head; the cheeks are blackish; chin white; breast rusty; belly, vent, and thighs pale buff; each wing is crossed by a white mark near the shoulder, and another smaller near the bastard wing; part of the tail, at the base, is white, the rest black; the two middle feathers wholly black, as are also the legs. The colours of the female are in general paler; the white streak over the eye, and the spots on the wings, are much less conspicuous; and the cheeks, instead of being black, partake of the colours of the head.

The Whinchat is a solitary bird, frequenting heaths and moors: it has no song, but only a simple unvaried note, and in manners very much resembles the Stonechat: it makes its nest very similar to that bird, and is generally seen in the same places during the summer months: the female lays five eggs, of a lightish blue, very faintly sprinkled with small rusty spots. In the northern parts of England it disappears in winter; but its migration is only partial, as it is seen in some of the southern counties at that season. It feeds on worms, flies and insects.

107

THE STONECHAT

Stone-smith, Moor-titling

(Motacilla Rubicola, Linn.—*Le Traquet,* Buff.*)*

Length nearly five inches. Bill black; eyes dark hazel; the head, neck, and throat black, faintly mixed with brown; on each side of the neck, immediately above the wings, there is a large white spot; the back and wing coverts are of a fine velvet black, margined with reddish brown; the quills are dusky, with pale brown edges, those next the body are white at the bottom, forming a spot of that colour on the wings; the breast is bay, lightest on the belly; the rump white; tail black, the outer feathers edged with rusty colour: legs black. The colours of the female are duller; the white on the sides of the neck is not so conspicuous; the breast and belly much paler, and the white spot on the rump is wanting.

This solitary bird is chiefly found on wild heaths and commons, where it feeds on small worms and insects of all kinds. They build at the roots of bushes, or underneath stones, carefully concealing the entrance to the nest by a variety of arts: it generally alights at some distance, and makes its approaches with great circumspection, creeping along the ground in a winding direction, so that it is a difficult matter to discover its retreat. They build about the end of March, and lay five or six eggs of a greenish pale blue. The flight of the Stonechat is low: it is almost continually on the wing, flying from bush to bush, alighting only for a few seconds. It remains with us the whole year, and in winter frequents moist places, in quest of food. Buffon compares its note to the word *wistrata* frequently repeated. Latham observes, that it seemed to him like the clicking of two stones together, from which circumstance it probably may have derived its name.

THE TITMOUSE
Ox-eye
(Parus major, Linn.*—La Grosse Mésange,* Buff.*)*

The length of this bird is about five inches. The bill and eyes are black; the head is covered apparently with a sort of hood, of a fine deep glossy black, which extends to the middle of the neck; cheeks white; belly greenish yellow, divided down the middle by a line of black reaching to the vent; the back is of an olive green; rump bluish grey; quills dusky, the greater edged with white, the lesser with pale green; the wing coverts are of a bluish ash; the greater coverts tipped with white, which forms a bar across the wings; the tail is black, the exterior edge of the outer feathers white: legs dark lead colour.

The Titmouse begins to pair early in February; the male and female consort for some time before they make their nest, composed of the softest materials and built generally in the hole of a tree: the female lays from eight to ten white eggs, spotted with rust colour. The young brood continue blind for several days, after which their growth is very rapid, and they are able to fly in about fifteen days: after they have quitted the nest they return no more to it, but perch on the neighbouring trees, and incessantly call on each other; they generally continue together till the approach of spring invites them to pair. We kept one of these birds in a cage for some time: it was fed chiefly with hemp-seed, which it held very dexterously in its claws, and pecked it till it broke the outside shell; it likewise ate raw flesh, minced small, and was very fond of flies, which when held to the cage, it seized avidly: it was continually in motion during the day, and would, for hours together, dart backwards and forwards. Its usual note was strong and simple; it had besides, a more varied, but very low song. During the night it rested on the bottom of the cage.

THE CRESTED TITMOUSE

(Parus cristatus, Linn.—*Le Mésange Huppée,* Buff.*)*

This shy and solitary species is rather more than four inches and a half in length. It is distinguished from the rest of the genus by having its head ornamented with a peaked crest of black feathers, narrowly margined with white; those beneath the crest and the brow are of the same colours, but the white greatly predominates. The bill and irides are dusky; the cheeks, and sides of the head and neck dull white; the chin, and fore part of the neck to the breast black; from thence a line of the same branches off, and bounding the white part of the neck, extends to the hinder part of the head; the auriculars, with the exception of a white spot in the middle, are black, and form a patch, which is pointed off towards the nape; the back and coverts are rusty dull brown; the quills and tail nearly the same, but more deeply tinged with rust colour; the breast, belly, and sides also partake of the same colours, but are much paler; the legs are lead colour, tinged with pale brown.

Some of the species have been met with in Scotland, but are considered rare visitants. They take up their abode in the deep recesses of forests, in various parts of the continent of Europe, and prefer the shelter of evergreen trees; but from their being of so retired a disposition, they are seldom seen there, even by the few whose business may lead them into these gloomy wilds. The above figure was made from a preserved specimen obligingly lent to this work by the Hon. H. T. Liddell, of Ravensworth Castle.

THE BLUE TITMOUSE

Tom-tit, Blue-cap, or Nun

(Parus cæruleus, Linn.—*La Mésange bleue,* Buff.*)*

The length of this beautiful bird is about four inches and a half. Bill and eyes black; crown of the head blue, terminated behind with a line of dirty white; sides of the head white, underneath which, from the throat to the hinder part of the neck, is a line of dark blue; from the bill, on each side, a narrow line of black passes through the eyes; the back is yellowish green; coverts blue, edged with white; quills black, with pale blue edges; tail blue, the two middle feathers longest; under parts of the body pale yellow: legs and claws black. The female is somewhat smaller than the male, has less blue on the head, and her colours in general are not so bright.

This busy little bird is seen frequently in our gardens and orchards, where its operations are much dreaded by the over-anxious gardener, who fears, that in its pursuit after its favourite food, which is often lodged in the tender buds, it may destroy them also, to the injury of the future harvest, not considering that it is the means of destroying a much more dangerous enemy, (the caterpillar) which it finds there: it has likewise a strong propensity to flesh, and is said to pick the bones of such small birds as it can master, as clean as skeletons. The female builds her nest in holes of walls or trees, which she lines well with feathers: she lays from fourteen to twenty white eggs, spotted with red. If her eggs should be touched, or one of them be broken, she forsakes her nest and builds again, but otherwise makes but one hatch in the year. This bird is distinguished above all the rest of the Titmice by its rancour against the Owl.

THE COAL TITMOUSE

(Parus ater, Linn.—La petite Charbonnière, Buff.)

This bird is somewhat less than the last, and weighs only two drachms; length four inches. Bill black, as are the head, throat, and part of the breast; from the corner of the bill, on each side, an irregular patch of white passes under the eyes, extending to the sides of the neck; a spot of the same occupies the hinder part of the head and neck; the back and all the upper parts are greenish ash; wing coverts tipped with white, which forms two bars across the wing; under parts reddish white: legs lead colour; tail somewhat forked at the end. This species frequents hilly woods, particularly those of the pine and fir, building in hollow trees, and laying eight or ten eggs of a pure white, with a few purple spots.

THE LONG-TAILED TITMOUSE

(Parus caudatus, Linn.—*La Mésange à longue queue,* Buff.*)*

Length nearly five inches and a half, of which the tail itself is rather more than three inches. Its bill is very short and black; eyes hazel; orbits red; top of the head white, mixed with grey: over each eye there is a broad black band, which extends backwards, and unites on the hinder part of the head, whence it passes down the back to the rump, bordered on each side with dull red; the cheeks, throat, and breast are white; the belly, sides, rump, and vent dull rose colour, mixed with white; the coverts of the wings are black, those next the body white, edged with rose; quills dusky, with pale edges: the tail consists of feathers of very unequal lengths; the four middle feathers are wholly black, the others white on the exterior edge: legs and claws black.

The nest of this bird is curious and elegant, of a long oval form, with a small entrance hole in the side, near the top; the outside is formed of moss, woven together with the silken shrouds of the aurelia of insects, and covered all over with lichens, fixed with the same silken material: from this thatch the rain trickles off without penetrating, whilst from its similarity in colour and appearance to the bark of the branch on which it is commonly placed, it is not easily discovered: the inside is thickly lined with a profusion of feathers, the soft webs of which are all laid inwards, with the quills or points stuck into the outward fabric. In this comfortable mansion the female deposits her sixteen or seventeen eggs, which are concealed almost entirely among the feathers: they are perfectly white,[1] but take a fine red blush from the transparency of the shell, which shows the yolk. This bird is not uncommon with us; its habits and places of resort are the same as those of the other Titmice. It flies very swiftly, and from its slender shape, and the great length of its tail, it seems like a dart shooting through the air. It is almost constantly in motion, running up and down the branches of trees with great facility. The young continue with the parents, and form little flocks through the winter: they utter a small shrill cry, only as a call, but in the spring their notes become more musical.

The Long-tailed Titmouse is found in northern Europe, and from the thickness of its coat, seems well calculated to bear the rigours of a severe climate.

---

1 *Eggs taken out of the same nest differ: some are delicately freckled with red spots. This difference of the eggs in the same nest is very common. At night the male and female roost in the nest: one with its tail out at the hole, and the other with its head. Their tails after incubation are very crooked and ruffled for a long time.* [Bewick's note]

THE BEARDED TITMOUSE

(Parus biarmicus, Linn.—*La Mésange barbue,* Buff.*)*

Length somewhat more than six inches. The bill is orange, but so delicate that it changes on the death of the bird to a dingy yellow; eyes also orange; head and back part of the neck pearl grey, or light ash; on each side of the head, from the eye, there is a black mark extending downwards on the neck, and ending in a point, not unlike a mustachio; the throat and fore part of the neck are silvery white; the back, rump, and tail light rust colour, as are the belly, sides, and thighs; the breast is delicate flesh red; the vent black; lesser coverts of the wings dusky, the greater rusty, with pale edges; the quills are dusky, edged with white, those next the body with rusty on the exterior web, and with white on the inner; the bastard wing is dusky, edged and tipped with white: legs black. The female wants the black mark on each side of the head; the crown of the head is rust colour, spotted with black; the vent feathers not black, but of the same colour as the belly.

The Bearded Titmouse is found chiefly in the southern parts of the kingdom; it frequents marshy places where reeds grow, on the seeds of which it feeds; it breeds there, though its minute history is imperfectly known. It is said, that they were first brought to this country from Denmark, by the Countess of Albemarle, and that some of them, having made their escape, founded a colony here; but Latham, with great probability, supposes that they are ours *ab origine,* and that it is owing to their frequenting the places where reeds grow, and which are not easily accessible, that so little is known of them. Edwards gives a figure of this bird, and describes it under the name of the Least Butcher Bird.

THE SWALLOW

Chimney or House Swallow

(Hirundo rustica, Linn.—L'Hirondelle domestique, Buff.)

Length somewhat more than six inches. Bill black; eyes hazel; forehead and chin red, inclining to chestnut; the whole upper part of the body black, reflected with purplish blue on the top of the head and scapulars; the quills of the wings, according to their position, are sometimes bluish black, and sometimes greenish brown, whilst those of the tail are black, with green reflections; the fore part of the breast is black, the rest of the breast and belly white; the inside and corners of the mouth yellow; tail very long and much forked, each feather, except the middle ones, marked with an oval white spot on the inner web: legs very short, delicately fine, and blackish. We have seen a young Swallow, which was shot on the 26th September; its length was scarcely five inches; its tail was short, and not forked; the feathers were black, wanting the white spots; its breast was tinged with red.

The Swallow makes its appearance soon after the vernal equinox, and leaves us again about the end of September: it builds generally in chimneys, in the inside, within a few feet of the top, or under the eaves of houses; the nest is curiously constructed, of a cylindrical shape, plastered with mud, mixed with straw and hair, and lined with feathers: it is attached to the sides or corners of the chimney, and is sometimes a foot in height, open at the top. The female lays five or six eggs, white, speckled with red. Swallows return to the same haunts: they build annually a new nest, and often fix it, if the place admit, above that occupied the preceding year. We are favoured by Sir John Trevelyan, Bart. with the following curious fact:—At Camerton Hall, near Bath, a pair of Swallows built their nest on the upper part of the frame of an old picture over the chimney,

coming through a broken pane in the window of the room. They came three years successively, and in all probability would have continued to do so if the room had not been put into repair, which prevented their access to it. Both this bird and the Martin have generally two broods in the year; the first in June, the other in August, or perhaps later. Swallows frequently roost at night, after they begin to congregate, by the sides of rivers and pools, from which circumstance it has been erroneously supposed that they retire into the water.

Not many attempts have been made to preserve Swallows alive during the winter, and of these, few have succeeded. The following experiments, by Mr James Pearson, of London, communicated to us by Sir John Trevelyan, Bart. are highly interesting, and throw great light upon the natural history of the Swallow; we shall give them nearly in Mr Pearson's own words.

Five or six of these birds were taken about the latter end of August, 1784, in a bat fowling-net, at night; they were put separately into small cages, and fed with Nightingale's food: in about a week or ten days they took food of themselves; they were then put altogether into a deep cage, four feet long, with gravel at the bottom; a broad shallow pan with water was placed in it, in which they sometimes washed themselves, and seemed much strengthened by it. One day Mr Pearson observed, that they went into the water with unusual eagerness, hurrying in and out again repeatedly, with such swiftness as if they had been suddenly seized with a frenzy. Being anxious to see the result, he left them to themselves about half an hour, and on going to the cage again, found them all huddled together in a corner, apparently dead; the cage was then placed at a proper distance from the fire, when only two of them recovered, and were as healthy as before – the rest died. The two remaining ones were allowed to wash themselves occasionally for a short time only; but their feet soon after became swelled and inflamed, which Mr P. attributed to their perching, and they died about Christmas; thus the

first year's experiment was in some measure lost. Not discouraged by the failure of this, Mr P. determined to make a second trial the succeeding year from a strong desire of being convinced of the truth respecting their going into a state of torpidity. Accordingly, the next season, having taken some more birds, he put them into the cage, and in every respect pursued the same methods as with the last; but to guard their feet from the bad effects of the damp and cold, he covered the perches with flannel, and had the pleasure to observe, that the birds throve extremely well; they sung their song through the winter, and soon after Christmas began to moult, which they got through without any difficulty, and lived three or four years, regularly moulting every year at the usual time. On the renewal of their feathers, it appeared, that their tails were forked exactly the same as in those birds which return hither in the spring, and in every respect their appearance was the same. These birds, says Mr Pearson, were exhibited to the society for promoting Natural History, on the 14th day of February, 1786, at the time they were in a deep moult, during a severe frost, when the snow was on the ground. Minutes of this circumstance were entered in the books of the society. These birds died at last from neglect, during a long illness which Mr Pearson had: they died in the summer. Mr P. concludes his very interesting account in these words:—'January 20, 1797, I have now in my house, No. 21, Great Newport-street, Long-Acre, four Swallows in moult, in as perfect health as any birds ever appeared to be when moulting.'

These experiments have since been amply confirmed by the observations of M. Natterer, of Vienna, as stated by M. Temminck in his *Manuel d'Ornithologie*; and the result clearly proves, what is in fact now admitted on all hands, that Swallows do not in any material instance differ from other birds in their nature and propensities; but that they leave us when this country can no longer furnish them with a supply of their proper and natural food; but more especially when the great object of their coming, that of propagating their kind, has been fulfilled.

THE MARTIN

Martlet, Martinet, or Window Swallow

(Hirundo urbica, Linn.*—L'Hirondelle à cul blanc,* Buff.*)*

Length about five inches and a half. Bill black; eyes dark hazel; inside of the mouth yellow; the top of the head, the wings, and tail dusky brown; back black, glossed with blue; the rump and all the under parts, from the chin to the vent, are pure white: ends of the secondary quill feathers finely edged with white; the legs are covered with white downy feathers down to the claws, which are white also, very sharp and much hooked; the middle toe is much longer than the others, and is connected with the inner one as far as the first joint.

This bird visits us in great numbers: it has generally two broods, sometimes three, in the year: it builds in craggy precipices near the sea, or by the sides of lakes, most frequently, however, under the eaves of houses,[1] or close by the window. The nest is made of mud and straw on the outside, and lined with feathers; the first hatch consists of five white eggs, dusky at the thicker end: the second of three or four; and the third of only two or three. While the young birds are confined to the nest, the parents feed them, adhering by the claws to the outside; but as soon as they are able to fly, they receive their nourishment on the wing, by a motion quick and almost imperceptible to those who are not accustomed to observe it.

The Martin arrives somewhat later than the Swallow, and does not leave us so soon: they have been observed in the neighbourhood of London so late as the middle of October. White, in his *Natural History of Selborne,* has made some judicious remarks on these birds, with a view to illustrate the time and manner of their migrations, to which, we beg leave to refer.

1 *The following passage of our 'sweet Shakespeare,' descriptive of its haunts, has always been admired as conveying a perfect idea of amenity of situation:—*

'The guest of summer,
The temple-haunting martlet, does approve
By his lov'd mansionry, that the heaven's breath
Smells wooingly here: no jutty, frieze, buttress,
Nor coigne of vantage, but this bird hath made
His pendent bed, and procreant cradle: Where they
Most breed and haunt, I have observed, the air
Is delicate.'
[Bewick's note.]

THE SAND MARTIN

Bank Martin, or Sand Swallow

(*Hirunda riparia, Linn.—L'Hirondelle de rivage, Buff.*)

Length about four inches and three quarters. Bill dark horn colour; the head, neck, breast, and back mouse colour; over each eye is a light streak; throat and fore part of the neck white, as are the belly and vent; the wings and tail brown; the feet smooth and dark brown.

This is the smallest, as well as the least numerous of our Swallows. It frequents the steep sandy banks of rivers, in the sides of which it makes deep holes, and places the nest at the end; it is carelessly constructed of straw, dry grass, and feathers; the female lays five or six white eggs, almost transparent, and is said to have only one brood in the year.

THE SWIFT

Black Martin, Deviling, or Screamer

(Hirundo Apus, Linn.—Le Martinet noir, Buff.)

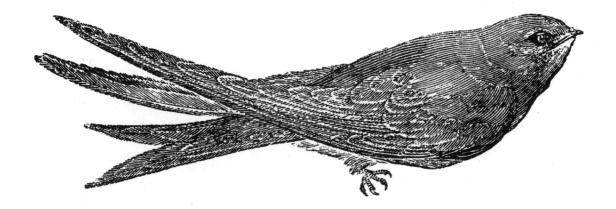

Length nearly eight inches. Bill black; eyes hazel; general colour a sooty black, with greenish reflections; throat white; wings long, measuring about eighteen inches tip to tip; tail much forked; legs dark brown, and very short; toes stand two and two on each side of the foot, and consist of two phalanges or joints only, a conformation peculiar to this bird. There is hardly any difference between the male and female.

The Swift arrives later, and departs sooner than any of the tribe: it is larger, stronger, and its flight is more rapid than that of any of its kindred. It has but one brood in the year, so that the young have time to gain strength enough to accompany the parents in their distant excursions. They have been noticed at the Cape of Good Hope, and probably visit the more remote regions of Asia. Swifts are almost continually on the wing; they fly higher, and wheel with bolder wing than the Swallows. The life of the Swift seems divided into two extremes; one of the most violent exertion, the other of perfect inaction; they must either shoot through the air, or remain close in their holes. They are seldom seen to alight; but if by any accident they should fall upon a piece of even ground, it is with difficulty they can recover themselves, owing to the shortness of their feet, and the great length of their wings. They are said to avoid heat, and for this reason pass the middle of the day in their holes; in the morning and evening they go out in quest of provision; they then are seen in flocks, describing an endless series of circles upon circles, all screaming together: they often glide along without stirring their wings, and on a sudden move them with frequent and quickly repeated strokes. Swifts build generally in lofty steeples and towers, sometimes under the arches of bridges: the nest is composed of a variety of materials, such as dry grass, moss, hemp, bits of cord, threads of silk, linen or muslin, feathers, and other light substances which they chance to find in the sweepings of towns. It is difficult to conceive how these birds, which are never seen to alight, gather such materials; some suppose that they catch them in the air as they are carried up by the wind; others, that they raise them by glancing along the surface of the ground; while others assert, with more probability, that they often rob the Sparrow, and occupy the same hole, after driving out the owner. The female lays five white eggs, rather pointed and spindle-shaped: the young ones are hatched about the latter end of May; they begin to fly about the middle of June, and shortly after abandon the nest, after which the parents seem no more to regard them.

Swifts begin to assemble previously to their departure, early in July: they soar higher, with shriller cries. These meetings continue till towards the middle of August, after which they disappear.

THE NIGHT-JAR

Goat-sucker, Dor-hawk, or Fern Owl

(Caprimulgus Europæus, Linn.—*L'Engoulivent,* Buff.*)*

Length is about ten inches and a half. Bill small, flat, and somewhat hooked at the tip, and furnished on each side of the upper mandible with several strong bristles, whereby it secures its prey; the lower jaw is edged with a white stripe, which extends backward towards the head; the eyes are large, full, and black; the plumage beautifully freckled and powdered with browns of various hues, mixed with rusty and white, but so diversified as to baffle all description. The male is distinguished by an oval spot of white on the inner webs of the first three quill feathers, and at the ends of the two outermost feathers of the tail; the legs are short, rough, and scaly, and feathered below the knee; the toes are connected by a membrane as far as the first joint; the middle one is considerably larger than the rest, and the claw is serrated on one side.

To avoid, as much as possible, perpetuating error, we have dropped the name Goat-sucker, which has no foundation but in ignorance and superstition, and have adopted one, which, though not universally known, bears some analogy to the nature and qualities of the bird, both with respect to the time of its appearance, which is always the dusk of the evening, as well as to the jarring noise which it utters whilst at rest perched on a tree, and by which it is peculiarly distinguished.

The Night-jar is found in every part of the old continent, from Siberia to Greece, Africa, and India; it arrives in this country about the end of May, being one of our latest birds of passage, and departs in the end of August or the beginning of September: it is nowhere numerous, and never appears in flocks. Like the Owl, it is seldom seen in the daytime, unless disturbed, or in dark and gloomy weather, when its eyes are not dazzled by the bright rays of the sun.

120

THE WILD PIGEON
Stock Dove
(Columba Œnas, Linn.—Le Biset, Buff.)

Length fourteen inches. Bill pale red; the head, neck, and upper back deep bluish grey, reflected on the sides of the neck with glossy green and gold; breast pale reddish purple; the lower part of the back and the rump light grey or ash, as are also the belly, thighs, and under tail coverts; the primary quill feathers are dusky, edged with white, the others grey, marked with two black spots on the exterior webs, forming two bars across each wing; tail ash grey, tipped black; lower half of the two outermost feathers white: legs and feet red; claws black. The Stock Dove, Rock Pigeon, and Wood Pigeon, with small differences, may be included under the same denomination, and are probably the origin of most of those beautiful varieties, which, in a state of domestication, are dependent upon man.

Wild Pigeons migrate in large flocks into England, at the approach of winter, from the northern regions, and return in the spring; many of them, however, remain in this country. They build in the hollows of decayed trees, and commonly have two broods in the year. In a state of domestication their fecundity is prodigious; and, though they never lay more than two eggs at a time, yet, allowing them to breed nine times in the year, the produce of a single pair, at the expiration of four years, may amount to the enormous number of 14,762. The male and female perform the office of incubation by turns, and feed their young by casting up the provisions out of their stomachs into the mouths of the young ones.

To describe the varieties of the domestic Pigeon would exceed the limits of our work. The Carrier Pigeon is the most deserving of notice, having been made use of, from very early times, to convey intelligence on the most important occasions, and it never fails to execute its commission with unequalled expedition and certainty.

THE TURTLE DOVE

(Columba Turtur, Linn.—La Tourterelle, Buff.)

Length somewhat more than twelve inches. Bill brown; eyes yellow, encompassed with a crimson circle; top of the head ash grey, mixed with olive; each side of the neck is marked with a spot of black feathers, tipped with white; the back is ash grey, each feather margined with reddish brown; wing coverts and scapulars reddish brown, spotted with black; quill feathers dusky, edges pale; the fore part of the neck and the breast are light purplish red; the belly, thighs, and vent white; the two middle feathers of the tail brown, the others dusky, tipped with white, the two outermost also edged with the same: legs red. One of these birds, which was sent us by the Rev. Henry Ridley, was shot out of a flock at Prestwick-Car, in Northumberland, in the month of September, 1794; it agreed in every respect with the Common Turtle, excepting the mark on each side of the neck, which was wholly wanting: we suppose it to have been a young bird.

The note of the Turtle Dove is singularly tender and plaintive: in addressing his mate, the male makes use of a variety of winning attitudes, cooing at the same time in the most gentle and soothing accents; on which account this bird has been represented in all ages, as the most perfect emblem of connubial attachment and constancy. It arrives late in the spring, and departs about the latter end of August: frequenting the thickest and most sheltered parts of the woods, where it builds on the highest trees: the female lays two eggs, and has only one brood in this country, but in warmer climates it is supposed to breed several times in the year. Turtles are pretty common in Kent, where they are sometimes seen in flocks of twenty or more, frequenting the pea fields, and doing much damage. Their stay with us seldom exceeds four or five months, during which time they pair, breed, and rear their young, which are strong enough to join them in their retreat.

THE COCK

(Phasianus Gallus, Linn.—*Le Coq*, Buff.*)*

The Cock, like the Dog, in his present state of domestication, differs so widely from his supposed wild original, as to render it a difficult matter to trace him back to his primitive stock; however it is generally agreed that he is to be found in a state of nature in the forests of India, and in most of the islands of the Indian seas. The varieties of this species are endless, every country and almost every district of each country, producing a different kind. From Asia, where they are supposed to have originated, they have been diffused over every part of the inhabited world. America was the last to receive them. It has been said that they were first introduced into Brazil by the Portuguese: they are now as common in all the inhabited parts of that vast continent as with us. Of those which have been selected for domestic purposes in this country, the principal are—

1. The Crested Cock, of which there are several varieties, such as the white-crested black ones; the black-crested white ones; the gold and silver ones, &c.

2. The Hamburgh Cock, named also Velvet Breeches, because its thighs and belly are of a soft black. This is a very large kind, much used for the table.

3. The Bantam, or Dwarf Cock, a diminutive but very spirited breed: its legs are furnished with long feathers, which reach to the ground behind; it is very courageous, and will fight with one much stronger than itself.

4. The Frizzled Cock. The feathers in this are so curled up that they seem to be reversed, and to stand in opposite directions. They are originally from the southern parts of Asia, and when young are extremely sensible of cold. They have a disordered and unpleasant appearance, but are in much esteem for the table.

5. The Silk Fowls, whose skin and bones are black. We shall finish our list with the English Game-cock, which stands unrivalled by those of any other country for its invincible courage, and on that account is made use of as the instrument of the cruel diversion of cockfighting. To trace this custom to its origin we must look back into ancient times. The Athenians allotted one day in the year to cockfighting; the Romans are said to have learned it from them; and by that warlike people it was first introduced into this island. Henry VIII was so attached to the sport, that in order to enjoy it, he caused a commodious house to he erected, which, though now applied to a very different purpose, still retains the name of the Cockpit.

The appearance of the Game-cock, when in his full plumage and not mutilated for the purpose of fighting, is strikingly beautiful and animated: his head, which is small, is adorned with a beautiful red comb, and his chin and throat with wattles; his eyes sparkle with fire, and his whole demeanor bespeaks boldness and freedom. The feathers on his neck are long, slender, and pointed, and fall gracefully down upon his body, which is thick, muscular, and compact; his tail is long, and the flexile feathers which fall over it form a beautiful arch behind, which gives a grace to all his motions: his legs are strong, and armed with sharp spurs, with which he defends himself and attacks his adversary; he lays hold with his beak, and strikes with the feet and wings. When surrounded by his females, his whole aspect is full of animation; he allows of no competitor, but on the approach of a rival, rushes forward to instant combat, and either drives him from the field, or perishes in the attempt. He is polygamous, but this is a habit probably forced upon him by domestication, for even in this state, there is always one female more favoured than the rest, yet he is very attentive to his seraglio; he leads, defends, and cherishes them, collects them together when they straggle, and eats unwillingly till he sees them feeding around him: when he loses them he utters his griefs aloud, and from the different inflections of his voice, and the various significant gestures which he makes, one would be led to conclude that it is a species of language which serves to communicate his sentiments. The fecundity of the hen is great; she lays generally two eggs in three days, and continues to lay through the greater part of the year, excepting the time of moulting, which lasts about two months. After having laid about ten or twelve eggs, she prepares for the anxious task of incubation, and gives the most certain indications of her wants by her cries and cluckings. Should she be deprived of her own eggs, she will cover those of any other kind, or even fictitious ones of stone or chalk. A sitting hen is a lively emblem of most affectionate solicitude; she covers her eggs with her wings and body, fosters them with a genial warmth, and changes them gently, that all parts may be properly heated: she seems to perceive the importance of her employment, on which she is so intent, that she apparently neglects, in some measure, the necessary supplies of food and drink; she omits no care, overlooks no precaution, to complete the existence of the little incipient beings, and to guard against the dangers that threaten them; the cock takes upon himself no part of the duty.

THE PHEASANT

(Phasianus Colchicus, Linn.—Le Faisan, Buff.)

Length two feet eleven inches. The bill is of a pale horn colour; the nostrils are hid under an arched covering; eyes yellow, and surrounded by a space in appearance like scarlet cloth, finely spotted with black; immediately under each eye is a small patch of short feathers of a dark glossy purple; the upper parts of the head and neck are deep purple, varying to green and blue; lower parts of the neck and the breast reddish chestnut, with black indented edges; the sides and lower part of the breast the same, with large tips of black to each feather, which in different lights vary to a glossy purple; the belly and vent are dusky; back and scapulars beautifully variegated with black and white, or cream colour speckled with black, and mixed with deep orange, all the feathers edged with black; on the lower part of the back is a mixture of green; the quills are dusky, freckled with white; wing coverts brown, glossed with green, and edged with white; rump plain reddish brown; the two middle feathers of the tail are about twenty inches long, the shortest on each side less than five, of a reddish brown, marked with bars of black: legs dusky, with a short blunt spur on each, but in some old birds the spurs are as sharp as needles; between the toes there is a strong membrane.

The female is less, and does not exhibit that variety and brilliancy of plumage: the general colours are light and dark brown, mixed with black, the breast and belly finely freckled with small black spots on a light ground; the tail is short, and barred somewhat; the space round the eye is covered with feathers.

Pheasants are generally found in low woody places, on the borders of plains, where they delight to sport: during the night they roost on tree branches. They are very shy birds, and do not associate together, except during the months of March and April, when the male seeks the female. The hen makes her nest on the ground and lays from twelve to fifteen olive-coloured eggs, smaller than those of the domestic Hen.

THE PEACOCK

(Pavo cristatus, Linn.—*Le Paon,* Buff.*)*

To describe the beauties of this bird, in adequate terms, would be a task of no small difficulty. 'Its matchless plumage,' says Buffon, 'seems to combine all that delights the eye in the soft and delicate tints of the finest flowers, all that dazzles it in the sparkling lustre of the gems, and all that astonishes it in the grand display of the rainbow.' Its head is adorned with a tuft, consisting of twenty-four feathers, whose slender shafts are furnished with webs only at the ends, painted with the most exquisite green, mixed with gold: the head, throat, neck, and breast, are of a deep blue glossed green and gold; the back of the same, tinged with bronze; the scapulars and lesser wing coverts reddish cream colour, variegated with black; the middle coverts deep blue, glossed green and gold; the greater coverts and bastard wing reddish brown, as are also the quills, some of which are variegated with black and green; the belly and vent are black, with a greenish hue; but the distinguishing character of this singular bird is its train, which rises above the tail, and, when erected, forms a fan of resplendent hues: the two middle feathers are sometimes four feet and a half long, the others gradually diminishing on each side; the white shafts are furnished from their origin nearly to the end, with parted filaments of varying colours ending in a flat vane, which is decorated with what is called the eye, a brilliant spot, enamelled with the most enchanting colours; yellow, gilded with various shades; green, running into blue and bright violet; the whole receiving additional lustre from the colour of the fine velvet black centre. When pleased, and in the sight of his females, the Peacock erects his train, and displays the majesty of his beauty.

The Peahen is less than the cock, and though furnished with a train and crest, is destitute of those beauties by which he is distinguished. She lays five or six whitish eggs, in some secret spot where she can conceal them from the male, who is apt to break them.

THE BLACK GROUSE

Black Game, or Black Cock

(Tetrao Tetrix, Linn.—Le Coq de Bruyère à queue fourchue, Buff.)

This bird, though not of greater bulk than the common Hen, weighs nearly four pounds: length about one foot ten inches, breadth two feet nine. The bill is dark; the eyes deep blue; below each eye is a spot of dirty white, and above a larger one, of a bright scarlet, which extends almost to the top of the head; the general colour of the plumage is deep black, richly glossed with blue on the neck and rump; the lesser wing coverts are dusky brown; the greater white, which extends to the ridge of the wing, forming a spot of that colour on the shoulder when the wing is closed; the quills are brown, the lower parts and tips of the secondaries white, forming a bar of white across the wing; the feathers of the tail are almost square at the ends, and when spread out, form a curve on each side; the under tail coverts are pure white: the legs and thighs dark brown, mottled white. In some of our specimens the nostrils were thickly covered with feathers, whilst in others they were quite bare, probably owing to the different ages of the birds.

These birds are common in Russia, Siberia, and other northern countries, chiefly in high and wooded situations; and in the northern parts of our own island on uncultivated moors: they feed on various kinds of berries and other fruits, the produce of wild and mountainous places: in summer they frequently come down from their lofty situations for the sake of feeding on corn.

The female is about one third less than the male, and differs from him considerably in colour; her tail is much less forked. She makes a nest on the ground, and lays from eight to twelve eggs, of a yellowish colour, with spots of a rusty brown. The young cocks at first resemble the mother, and do not acquire their male garb till towards the end of autumn, when their plumage gradually changes to a deeper colour.

THE RED GROUSE

Red Game, Moor Game, Gorcock, or Moor Cock

(Tetrao Scoticus, Linn.—L'Attagas, Buff.)

The length of this bird is fifteen inches; weight about nineteen ounces. The bill is black; the eyes hazel; nostrils shaded with small red and black feathers; at the base of the lower bill is a white spot on each side; the throat is red; each eye arched with a large naked spot, of a bright scarlet; the upper part of the body mottled with deep red and black, which gives it the appearance of tortoise-shell; the breast and belly purplish, crossed with small dusky lines; the tail is of sixteen feathers, of equal lengths, the four middle ones barred with red, the others black; quills dusky; the legs are clothed with soft white feathers down to the claws, which are strong, and of a light colour. The female is somewhat less and the colours of her plumage are much lighter than those of the male.

This bird is found in great plenty in the wild, heathy, and mountainous tracts in the northern counties of England and Wales, and particularly in the Highlands of Scotland. It is peculiar to Britain; those found in the mountainous parts of France, Spain, Italy, and elsewhere are probably only varieties of this kind, and no doubt would breed with it. It is to be wished that attempts were more frequently made to introduce a greater variety of these useful birds into this country, to stock our barren moors with a rich fund of delicate and wholesome food; but till the legislature shall alter our very unequal and injudicious game laws, there hardly remains a single hope for the preservation of such birds of this species as we now have.

Red Grouse pair in the spring: the female lays eight or ten eggs on the ground. The young ones follow the hen the whole summer: as soon as they have attained their full size, they unite in flocks of forty or fifty, and are then exceedingly shy and wild.

THE PARTRIDGE

(Tetrao Perdix, Linn.—*La Perdrix Grise*, Buff.*)*

Length about thirteen inches. Bill light brown: eyes hazel; the general colour of its plumage is brown and ash, beautifully mixed with black; each feather streaked down the middle with buff; the sides of the head are tawny; under each eye is a small saffron-coloured spot and between the eye and the ear naked skin of a bright scarlet, which is not very conspicuous but in old birds; on the breast there is a crescent of a deep chestnut; the tail is short and drooping: the legs are greenish white, and furnished with a small knob behind. The female has no crescent on the breast, and her colours in general are not so distinct and bright as those of the male. The moult takes place once a year.

Partridges are found chiefly in temperate climates; they are nowhere in greater plenty than in this island, where, in their season, they contribute to our entertainments. They pair early in the spring, and once united it is rare that anything but death separates them: the female lays from fourteen to eighteen or twenty eggs, making her nest of dry leaves and grass upon the ground. The young birds run as soon as hatched, frequently encumbered with part of the shell. It is no unusual thing to introduce Partridge's eggs under the Common Hen, who hatches and rears them as her own.

The affection of the Partridge for her young is strong and lively; she is greatly assisted in the care of rearing them by her mate: they lead them out in common, call them together, gather for them their proper food, and assist in finding it by scratching the ground; they frequently sit close by each other, covering the chicks with their wings, like the Hen. In this situation they are not easily flushed; the sportsman attentive to the preservation of his game will avoid disturbing them, but should the pointer come too near the male first gives the signal of alarm by a peculiar cry of distress, throwing himself immediately in the way of danger, to deceive the enemy; he runs along the ground, hanging his wings, and exhibiting every symptom of debility, whereby the dog is decoyed, in the too eager expectation of an easy prey, to a distance from the covey; the female flies off in a contrary direction, and to a greater distance, but returning soon after by secret ways, she finds her scattered brood closely squatted among the grass, and leads them from the danger, before the dog has had time to return from his pursuit.

THE GREAT BUSTARD

(Otis Tarda, Linn.—*L'Outarde,* Buff.*)*

This very singular bird, which is the largest of our land birds, is about four feet long, and weighs from twenty-five to thirty pounds. The bill is strong, and rather convex; the eyes red; on each side of the root of the lower mandible there is a tuft of feathers about nine inches long; the head and neck are ash-coloured. The back is barred with black and bright rusty on a pale reddish ground; the quills are black; belly white: the tail consists of twenty feathers; the middle ones are rufous, barred with black; those on each side are white, with a bar or two of black near the ends: the legs are long, naked above the knees, and dusky; it has no hind toe; the nails are short, strong, and convex both above and below; the bottom of the foot is furnished with a callous prominence, which serves instead of a heel. The female is not much more than half the size of the male: the top of her head is deep orange, the rest of the head brown; her colours are not so bright as those of the male, and she has no tufts on the head. There is another difference between the male and female: the former has a pouch in the fore part of the neck, capable of containing about two quarts; the entrance is immediately under the tongue. This was discovered by Dr Douglas, who supposes that the bird fills it with water as a supply in the midst of those dreary plains where it is accustomed to wander; it makes a further use of it in defending itself against the attacks of birds of prey, throwing out the water with such violence as to baffle its enemy.

The female builds no nest, but making a hole on the ground, drops two eggs, about the size of those of a Goose, of a pale olive brown, with dark spots.

THE LITTLE BUSTARD

(Otis Tetrax, Linn.—La petite Outarde, Buff.)

Length seventeen inches. The bill is pale brown; irides red; the top of the head black, spotted with pale rusty: the sides of the head, the chin, and throat, reddish white, marked with a few dark spots; the whole neck in the male is black, encircled with an irregular band of white near the top and bottom; the back and wings rufous, mottled with brown, and crossed with fine irregular black lines; the under parts of the body, and outer edges of the wings, are white: the tail consists of eighteen feathers; the middle ones tawny, barred with black, the others white, marked with a few irregular bands of black: legs grey. The female (from which our figure was taken) differs from this description, is smaller, and has not the black collar; in other respects she nearly resembles the male.

This bird is very uncommon in this country; and we have seen only two, both of them females. The figure was drawn from one sent by W. Trevelyan, Esq. which was taken on the edge of Newmarket Heath, and kept alive about three weeks in a kitchen, where it was fed with bread and other things, such as poultry eat. It is common in France, where it is taken in nets like the Partridge. It is a very shy and cunning bird; if disturbed, it flies two or three hundred paces, not far from the ground, and then runs away much faster than anyone can follow on foot. The female lays in June, to the number of three or four eggs, of a glossy green: as soon as the young are hatched, she leads them about as the Hen does her chickens: they begin to fly about the middle of August.

Both this and the Great Bustard are excellent eating, and would well repay the trouble of domestication; indeed it seems surprising that we should suffer these fine birds to be in danger of total extinction, although, if properly cultivated, they might afford as excellent a repast as our own domestic poultry, or even as the Turkey, for which we are indebted to distant countries.

THE GOLDEN PLOVER

Yellow Plover

(Charadrius Pluvialis, Linn.—*Le Pluvier doré,* Buff.*)*

Length ten inches. Bill dusky; eyes dark; all the upper parts of the plumage are marked with bright yellow spots upon a dark brown ground; the fore part of the neck and the breast are the same, but much paler; the belly is almost white; the quills are dusky; the tail is marked with dusky and yellow bars; the legs are black. Birds of this species vary much from each other; in some which we have had, the breast was marked with black and white; in others, it was almost black; but whether this difference arose from age or sex, we are at a loss to determine.

The Golden Plover is common in this country and all the northern parts of Europe; it is very numerous in various parts of America, from Hudson's Bay as far as Carolina, migrating from one place to another, according to the seasons. It breeds on high and heathy mountains: the female lays four eggs, of a pale olive colour, variegated with blackish spots. They fly in small flocks, and make a shrill whistling noise, by an imitation of which they are sometimes enticed within gunshot. The male and female do not differ from each other. In young birds the yellow spots are not very distinguishable, as the plumage inclines more to grey.

THE DOTTEREL

(Charadrius Morinellus, Linn.—*Le Guignard*, Buff.*)*

Length about nine inches. The bill is black; eyes dark, large and full; forehead mottled with brown and white; the top of the head black; over each eye an arched line of white passes to the hinder part of the neck; the cheeks and the throat are white; the back and the wings light brown, inclining to olive, each feather margined with pale rust; the quills are brown; the fore part of the neck is surrounded by a broad band of a light olive, bordered on the under side with white; the breast is pale dull orange; the middle of the belly black; the rest of the belly, thighs, and vent reddish white; the tail is olive brown, black near the end, and tipped with white, the outer feathers are margined with white: legs dark olive.

The Dotterel is common in various parts of Great Britain, though in some places it is scarcely known. They are supposed to breed in the mountains of Cumberland and Westmoreland, where they are sometimes seen in the month of May; they likewise breed on several of the Highland hills: they are very common in Cambridgeshire, Lincolnshire, and Derbyshire, appearing in small flocks on the heaths and moors of those counties during the months of May and June, and are then very fat, and much esteemed for the table.

THE SANDERLING
Towillee, or Curwillet
(Charadrius Calidris, Linn.—Maubeche, Buff.)

This bird weighs almost two ounces; is about eight inches in length, and fifteen in breadth, from tip to tip. The bill is an inch long, slender, black and grooved on the sides nearly from the tip to the nostril; the brow to the eyes white; rest of the head pale ash grey, mottled in brown streaks from the forehead to the hinder part of the neck, and on each side of the upper part of the breast; back, scapulars, and greater coverts, brownish ash, edged with dull white, and irregularly marked with dark brown spots. The pinions, lesser coverts and bastard wings, dark brown; the quills, which extend beyond the tail, are of the same colour on their exterior webs and points, except four of the middle ones, which are white on the outer webs, forming, when the wing is closed, a sharp wedge-shaped spot; inner webs brownish ash; secondary quills brown, tipped with white; the rump and tail coverts also brown, edged with dirty white; tail feathers brownish ash, edged with a lighter shade, the two middle ones much darker than the rest; throat, fore part of the neck, breast, belly, thighs and vent white; the toes and legs black, and bare a little above the knees. This bird is of a slender form, and its plumage has a hoary appearance among the Stints, with which it associates on the seashore, in various parts of Great Britain. It wants the hinder toe, and has, in other respects, the look of the Plover and Dotterel, to which family it belongs.

Latham says, this bird, like the Purre, and some others, varies considerably, either from age or the season; for those he received in August, had the upper parts dark ash-coloured, and the feathers deeply edged with a ferruginous colour; but others sent him in January were of a plain dove-coloured grey; they differed also in some other trifling particulars.

WATER BIRDS

THE CRANE
Common Crane
(Ardea Grus, Linn.—*La Grue*, Buff.*)*

The bill is about four inches long, straight, pointed, and compressed at the sides, of a greenish black, lighter towards the point; tongue broad and short, and horny on the tip. The forehead, to the middle of the crown, is covered with black hairy down, through which the skin appears red; behind this it is nearly bare, and entirely so for the space of about two inches on the nape of the neck, which is ash grey. The sides of the head behind the eyes, and the hinder part of the neck, are white. The space between the bill and eyes, the cheeks, and fore part of the neck, are blackish; greater wing coverts also blackish, and those farthest from the body, with the bastard wing and quills, quite black: the rest of the plumage is a fine waved light ash. From the pinion of each wing springs an elegant tuft of loose feathers, curled at the ends, which fall over the tail, in their flexibility, position, and texture, resembling the plumes of the Ostrich. The legs and bare part of the thighs are black. The Crane measures, when extended, from the tip of the bill to the toes, more than five feet in length, and weighs nearly ten pounds; its gait is erect, and its figure tall and slender.

The Crane differs from the Stork and Heron in the singular conformation of the windpipe, which, entering the breast bone and being thrice reflected, goes out again at the same hole, and so turns down to the lungs. It differs from them also in some other particulars.

This species performs the boldest and most distant journeys. In summer they spread over the north of Europe and Asia as far as the Arctic Circle, and in winter are met with in India, Syria, &c. and the Cape of Good Hope. Their flight is discovered by the loud noise they make, for they may soar to such a height as to be hardly visible to the naked eye.

THE STORK

White Stork

(Ardea Ciconia, Linn.*—La Cicogne,* Buff.*)*

The Stork is smaller than the Crane, but much larger than the Heron: the length, from the point of the bill to the end of the tail, is three feet six inches; and its breadth, from tip to tip, above six feet. The bill is a fine red, and its length seven inches; the legs and bare part of the thighs are also red. The plumage is of a bright white, except the quills, greater coverts, and some of the scapulars, which are black; eyes dark and full, the orbits bare of feathers, and of a dusky reddish hue. The neck is long and arched; the feathers near the breast long and pendulous; secondary quills nearly of the same length as the primaries, and when the wings are closed, they cover its short tail. The female nearly resembles the male. The nest is made of dry sticks, twigs, and aquatic plants, sometimes on large trees or high cliffs: this, however, seldom happens, for the stork prefers the neighbourhood of populous places, where it finds protection from the inhabitants; who, for ages, have regarded both the bird and its nests as sacred, and commonly place boxes for them on the tops of the houses wherein to make their nests; to which they return after the most distant journeys, and every Stork takes possession of his own box. When these are not provided for them, they build on the tops of chimneys, steeples, and lofty ruins.

The Stork lays from two to four eggs, the size and colour of those of a Goose, and the male and female sit by turns. They are singularly attentive to their young; the nest is watched by one of them, while the other is seeking for provisions. Their food consists of lizards, frogs, small fish, &c. for which they watch with a keen eye, on the margins of lakes and pools, and in swamps and marshes. In low countries abounding with such places, such as Holland, the Stork is a welcome visitant. In its migrations this bird avoids the extremes of heat and cold: in summer it is never seen farther north than Sweden or Russia, and in winter it is not known to venture further south than Egypt.

THE HERON

Common Heron, Heronsewgh, or Heronshaw

(Ardea Major, Linn.—Le Heron huppé, Buff.)

Although the Heron is of a long, lank, awkward shape, yet its plumage gives it on the whole an agreeable appearance; but when stripped of its feathers, it looks as if it had been starved to death. It seldom weighs more than between three and four pounds, notwithstanding it measures about three feet in length, and in its breadth, from tip to tip, above five. The bill is six inches long, straight, pointed, and strong, and its edges are thin and slightly serrated; the upper mandible is of a yellowish horn colour, darkest on the ridge; the under one yellow. A bare greenish skin is extended from the beak beyond the eyes, the irides of which are yellow, and give them a fierce and piercing aspect. The brow and crown of the head are white, bordered above the eyes by black lines which reach the nape of the neck, where they join a long flowing pendent crest of the same colour. The upper part of the neck, in some, is white, in others pale ash; the fore part, lower down, is spotted with a double row of black feathers, and those which fall over the breast are long, loose, and unwebbed; the shoulders and scapular feathers are of the same texture, of a grey colour, generally streaked with white, and spread over its down-clothed back. The ridge of the wing is white, coverts and secondaries lead grey, bastard wings and quills bluish black, as are also the long soft feathers which take their rise on the sides under the wings, and, falling down, meet at their tips, and hide all the under parts: the latter, next the skin, are covered with a thick, matted, dirty white down, except about the belly and vent, which are almost bare. The tail is short, and consists of twelve feathers of a cinereous or brownish lead colour; the legs are dirty green, long, bare above the knees, and the middle claw is jagged on the inner edge.

The female has not the long flowing crest, or the long feathers which hang over the breast of the male, and her whole plumage is more uniformly dull and obscure. In the breeding season they congregate in large societies, and, like the Rooks, build their nests on trees, with sticks, lined with dried grass, wool, and other warm materials. The female lays from four to six eggs, of a pale greenish blue colour.

This bird is of a melancholy deportment, a silent and patient creature; in the most severe weather it will stand motionless a long time in the water, with its head laid back between its shoulders, its bill overlapped by the long feathers of the neck, as a defence from the cold, and fixed to a spot, in appearance, like the stump or root of a tree, waiting for its prey, which consists of eels and other kinds of fish, frogs, water-newts, &c.; it is also said to devour field-mice.

The Heron traverses the country to a great distance in quest of some convenient fishing spot, and in its aerial journeys soars to a great height, to which the eye is directed by its harsh cry, uttered from time to time while on the wing. In flying it draws the head between the shoulders, and the legs stretched out, seem, like the longer tails of some birds, to serve as a rudder. The motion of their wings is heavy and flagging, and yet they get forward at a greater rate than would be imagined.

In England Herons were formerly ranked among the royal game, and protected as such by the laws; and whoever destroyed their eggs was liable to a penalty of twenty shillings for each offence. Heron hawking was at that time a favourite diversion among the nobility and gentry of the kingdom, at whose tables this bird was a favourite dish, and was as much esteemed as Pheasants and Peacocks.

1 *A remarkable circumstance, with respect to these birds, occurred not long ago, at Dallam Tower, in Westmoreland, the seat of Daniel Wilson, Esq.*

There were two groves adjoining to the park: one of which, for many years, had been resorted to by a number of Herons, which there built and bred; the other was one of the largest rookeries in the country. The two tribes lived together for a long time without any disputes. At length the trees occupied by the Herons, consisting of some very fine old oaks, were cut down in the spring of 1775, and the young brood perished by the fall of the timber. The parent birds immediately set about preparing new habitations, in order to breed again; but, as the trees in the neighbourhood of their old nests were only of late growth, and sufficiently high to secure them from the depredation of boys, they determined to effect a settlement in the rookery. The Rooks made an obstinate resistance; but, after a very violent contest, in the course of which many of the Rooks, and some of their antagonists, lost their lives, the Herons at last succeeded in their attempt, built their nests, and brought out their young.

The next season the same contests took place, which terminated like the former, by the victory of the Herons. Since that time peace seems to have agreed upon them: the Rooks have relinquished possession of that part of the grove which the Herons occupy; the Herons confine themselves to those trees they first seized upon, and the two species live together in as much harmony as they did before their quarrel.— Heysham. [Bewick's note.]

THE LITTLE EGRET

(Ardea Garzetta, Linn.—L'Aigrette, Buff.)

The Egret is one of the smallest, as well as the most elegant of the Heron tribe: its shape is delicate, and the plumage white as snow; but what constitutes its principal beauty, are the soft, silky, flowing plumes on the head, breast, and shoulders; they consist of single slender shafts, thinly set with pairs of fine soft threads, which float on the slightest breath of air. Those which arise from the shoulders are extended over the back, and flow beyond the tail. These plumes were formerly used to decorate the helmets of warriors: they are now applied to a gentler and better purpose, in ornamenting the headdresses of the European ladies, and the turbans of the Persians and Turks.

The Egret seldom exceeds a pound and a half in weight, and rarely a foot and a half in length. A bare green skin is extended from the beak to the eyes, the irides are pale yellow: the bill and legs black. Like the common Heron they perch and build on trees, and live on the same kinds of food.

This species is found in almost every temperate and warm climate, and must formerly have been plentiful in Great Britain, if it be the same bird as that mentioned by Leland in the list or bill of fare prepared for the famous feast of Archbishop Nevil, in which one thousand of these birds were served up. No wonder the species has become nearly extinct in this country!

THE BITTERN

Bog-bumper, Bitter-bum, or Mire-drum

(Ardea Stellaris, Linn.—*Le Butor,* Buff.*)*

The Bittern is nearly as large as the Heron; but its legs are stronger, body more plump and fleshy, and its neck more thickly feathered. The beak is strong at the base, straight, and tapers to an acute point; the upper mandible is brown, the under inclining to green; the gape extends beyond the eyes, with a dusky patch at each angle: irides yellow. The crown of the head is covered with long black feathers; throat yellowish white, sides of the neck pale rusty, variegated with black, and on the fore part the ground colour is whitish, and the feathers fall down in less broken and darker lengthened stripes. These neck feathers, which it can raise and depress at pleasure, are long and cover the neck behind; those below them on the breast, to the thighs, are streaked with black, edged with yellowish white: the thighs, belly, and vent are dull pale yellow, clouded with dingy brown. The plumage has lines, bars and streaks, upon a ground shaded with rufous and yellow. The tail, which has ten feathers, is very short: the legs are pale green, bare a little above the knees; the claws are long and sharp. The female is less than the male; her plumage is darker, and the feathers on the head, breast, and neck are shorter. She makes an artless nest, composed chiefly of the withered stalks and leaves of the high coarse herbage, and lays from four to six eggs of a greenish white.

The Bittern is a shy, solitary bird with a singularly resounding cry which it utters from time to time while on the wing; but this cry is feeble when compared to the hollow booming noise which it makes during the night, in the breeding season, from its swampy retreats.

THE LITTLE BITTERN

(Ardea minuta, Linn.—*Le Blongios*, Buff.*)*

The body is about the size of a Thrush. The bill from the tip to the brow is in length one inch and seven eighths, greenish yellow, dusky at the tip of the upper mandible, and the edges are jagged; the feathers on the top of the head are elongated behind; these, as well as the back and tail are black, with greenish reflections, and the secondary and primary quills are nearly the same; the neck is long, the hinder part of it bare of feathers, but those from the fore part fall back and cover it; sides of the chin dull white; the cheeks incline to chestnut; the neck, lesser coverts of the wings, lower part of the breast, and the thighs, are reddish buff; greater coverts white; the belly and vent yellowish dirty white; the feathers on the upper part of the breast are black, edged with pale buff, and are spread over part of the shoulders, breast, and wings; those below, which cover the breast to the thighs, are long and narrowly striped down the middle with pale brown; legs and toes dark green, and nearly of the same length as the bill.

This species is very rarely met with in this country. The above figure was taken from a stuffed specimen, obligingly lent to this work by Sir M. W. Ridley, Bart. of Blagdon, Northumberland: the bird was shot there on the 10th of May, 1810.

THE SPOONBILL
White Spoonbill
(Platalea Leucorodia, Linn.—Le Spatule, Buff.)

The Spoonbill measures two feet eight inches in length. The whole plumage is white, though a few have been noticed with the quills tipped with black.

The bill, which flaps together not unlike two pieces of leather, is the most striking feature: it is six inches and a half long, broad and thick at the base, and very flat towards the extremity, where it is widened and rounded like a spatula: it is rimmed with black, and terminated with a small downward-bent point. The colour of the bill varies in different birds; in some, the little ridges which wave across the upper bill are spotted, in others striped with black or brown, and generally the ground colour of both mandibles is deeper or lighter yellow: the insides, near the edges, are studded with small hard tubercles or furrowed prominences, and are also rough near the extremities of the bill, which enables them to hold their slippery prey. A black bare skin extends from the bill round the eyes, the irides of which are grey; the skin which covers the gullet is also black and bare, and is capable of great distention. The feathers on the hinder part of the head form a sort of tuft or crest which falls behind. The toes are connected near their junction by webs: the feet, legs and bare part of the thighs are covered with a hard and scaly skin of a dirty black.

The Spoonbill migrates north in the summer, and returns south on the approach of winter, and is seen in all the intermediate low countries, between the Faroe Isles and the Cape of Good Hope. In England they are rare visitants. They build their nests on the tops of large trees, and lay three or four eggs, the size of those of a Hen, white, sprinkled with pale red.

THE CURLEW

(Scolopax arquata, Linn.—*Le Courlis,* Buff.*)*

The Curlew generally measures about two feet in length, and from tip to tip above three feet. The bill is about seven inches long, of a regular curve, and tender substance at the point, which is blunt. The upper mandible is black, gradually softening into brown towards the base; the under one flesh-coloured. The head and neck are streaked with darkish and light brown; wing coverts the same; the feathers of the back and scapulars are nearly black in the middle, edged and deeply indented with pale rust or light grey. The breast, belly, and lower part of the back are dull white, the latter thinly spotted with black, the two former with oblong strokes more thickly set, of the same colour. The quill feathers are black, the inner webs crossed or spotted with white: tail barred with black, on a white ground tinged with red: thighs bare about halfway above the knees, of a bluish colour; the toes are thick, and flat on the under side, being furnished with membraneous edgings on each side to the claws.

The female is so nearly like the male, that any particular description of her is unnecessary: she makes her nest upon the ground, in a dry tuft of rushes or grass, of such withered materials as are found near, and lays four eggs of a greenish cast, spotted with brown.

The Curlew is met with in most parts of Europe, from Iceland to the Mediterranean Islands. In Britain their summer residence is upon the large, heathy, and boggy moors, where they breed. Their food consists of worms, flies, and insects, which they pick out of the soft mossy ground by the marshy pools, which are common in such places. In autumn and winter they depart to the seaside, in great numbers, and there live upon worms, marine insects, and other fishy substances which they pick up on the beach, and among the loose rocks and pools left by the retiring tide.

THE WOODCOCK

(Scolopax Rusticola, Linn.—*La Bécasse,* Buff.*)*

The Woodcock measures fourteen inches in length, twenty-six in breadth, and weighs about twelve ounces. The shape of the head is obtusely triangular, with the eyes placed near the top, and the ears very forward. The upper mandible, which measures about three inches, is furrowed nearly its whole length, and at the tip it projects beyond and hangs over the under one, ending in a kind of knob, which is susceptible of the finest feeling, and calculated by that means, aided, perhaps, by an acute smell, to find the small worms in the soft moist grounds, from whence it extracts them with its sharp-pointed tongue. With the bill it also turns over fallen leaves in search of insects. The crown of the head is ash colour; the nape and back part of the neck are black, marked with three bars of rusty red: a black line extends from the corners of the mouth to the eyes, the orbits of which are pale buff; the whole under parts are yellowish white, numerously barred with dark waved lines. The tail consists of twelve feathers, which are black, and indented across with reddish spots on the edges: the tip is ash above, and glossy white below. The legs are short, feathered to the knees, and, in some, are bluish, in others, sallow flesh colour. The upper parts of the plumage are marbled, spotted, barred, streaked, and variegated; the colours, consisting of black, white, grey, red, brown, rufous, and yellow, are so disposed in rows, crossed and broken at intervals by lines and marks of different shapes, that the whole seems to the eye, at a little distance, blended together, which makes the bird appear exactly like the withered stalks and leaves of ferns, sticks, moss, and grasses, which form the background of its scenery.

The Woodcock is migratory, and leaves the countries bordering upon the Baltic in the autumn on its route to this country. They drop in upon our shores singly or in pairs, from the beginning of October till December. The female makes her nest on the ground, generally at the root or stump of a decayed tree; it is carelessly formed of dried fibres and leaves, upon which she lays four or five eggs, larger than those of a Pigeon, of a rusty grey, blotched and marked with dusky spots.

THE SNIPE
Snite, or Heather-bleater

(Scolopax Gallinago, Linn.—*La Bécassine,* Buff.)

The Snipe is generally about four ounces in weight, twelve inches in length, and fourteen in breadth. The bill is nearly three inches long, pale brown or greenish yellow, flat and dark at the tip, and smooth: the head is divided lengthwise by three reddish or rusty white lines, and two of black; one of the former passes along the middle of the crown, and one above each eye: a darkish mark is extended from the corners of the mouth nearly to each eye, and the auriculars form spots of the same colour: the chin and fore part of the neck are yellowish white, the former plain, the latter spotted with brown. The scapulars are striped lengthwise on one web, and barred on the other, with black and yellow: quills dusky, the edge of the primaries, and tips of the secondaries, white; those next to the back barred with black, and pale rufous: the breast and belly are white: the tail coverts are reddish brown, and so long as to cover the greater part of it; the tail consists of fourteen feathers, the webs of which, as far as they are concealed by the coverts, are dusky, thence downward, tawny or rusty orange, and irregularly marked or crossed with black. The tip is commonly of a pale reddish yellow, but in some specimens nearly white: the legs are pale green.

The common residence of the Snipe is in small bogs or wet grounds, where it digs and nibbles in the soft mud, in search of its food, which consists chiefly of a very small red transparent worm; it is said also to eat slugs, insects, and grubs, which breed in great abundance in those slimy stagnant places.

Numbers of Snipes leave Great Britain in the spring, and return in the autumn, yet many constantly remain and breed in various parts of the country. The female makes her nest in the most retired and inaccessible part of the morass, generally under the stump of an alder or willow: it is composed of withered grasses and a few feathers: her eggs, four or five in number, are of an oblong shape, and greenish, with rusty spots.

THE GODWIT

Common Godwit, Godwyn, Yarwhelp, or Yarwip

(Scolopax ægocephala, Linn.*—La grande Barge grise,* Buff.*)*

The weight of this bird is about twelve ounces; length about sixteen inches. Bill four inches long, and bent a little upwards, black at the point, gradually softening into a pale purple towards the base; a whitish streak passes from the bill over each eye: the head, neck, back, scapulars, and coverts, are dingy reddish pale brown, each feather marked down the middle with a dark spot. The fore part of the breast is streaked with black; belly, vent, and tail white, the latter regularly barred with black: the webs of the first six quill feathers black, edged on the interior sides with reddish brown: legs in general dark coloured, inclining to greenish blue.

The Godwit is met with in various parts of Europe, Asia, and America: in Great Britain, in the spring and summer, it resides in the fens and marshes, where it rears its young, and feeds upon small worms and insects. During these seasons it removes only from one marsh to another; but when the winter sets in with severity, it seeks the salt marshes and seashores.

1 *The Godwit is much esteemed, by epicures, as a great delicacy, and sells very high. It is caught in nets, to which it is allured by a stale, or stuffed bird, in the same manner, and in the same season, as the Ruffs and Reeves. [Bewick's note.]*

THE GREENSHANK

Green-shanked Godwit, or Green-legged Horseman

(Scolopax glottis, Linn.—La Barge variée, Buff.)

The Greenshank is of a slender and elegant shape, and its weight small in proportion to its length and dimensions, being only about six ounces, although it measures from the tip of its beak to the end of its tail fourteen inches, and to the toes twenty; and from the tip to tip of the wings, twenty-five. The bill is about two inches and a half long, straight and slender, the upper mandible black, the under reddish at its base. The upper parts of its plumage are pale brownish ash, but each feather is marked down the shaft with a glossy bronze brown: the under parts, and rump, are pure white: a whitish streak passes over each eye: the quill feathers are dusky, plain on the outer webs, but the inner ones are speckled with white spots: the tail is white, crossed with dark waved bars: the legs long, bare about one inch above the knees, and dark green: the outer toe is connected by a membrane to the middle one as far as the first joint.

This species is not numerous in England, but they appear in small flocks, in the winter season, on the seashores and the adjacent marshes; their summer residence is the northern regions of Russia, Siberia, &c. They are also met with in various parts of both Asia and America. Their flesh, like all the rest of this genus, is well-flavoured, and esteemed good eating.

The above figure and description were taken from a stuffed specimen in the Newcastle Museum. Annexed is one of the tail feathers.

THE REDSHANK

Red-legged Horseman, Pool Snipe, or Sand Cock

(Scolopax Calidris, Linn.—Le Chevalier aux Pieds Rouges, Buff.)

This bird weighs about five ounces and a half: the length is twelve inches, breadth twenty-one. The bill is more than an inch and three quarters long, black at the point, and red towards the base: the feathers on the crown of the head are dark brown, edged with pale rufous; a light or whitish line passes over, and surrounds each eye, from the corners of which a dark brown spot is extended to the beak: irides hazel: hinder part of the neck obscurely spotted with dark brown, on a rusty ash ground; throat and fore part more distinctly marked or streaked with spots of the same colour: on the breast and belly, which are white, tinged with ash, the spots are thinly distributed, and are shaped something like the heads of arrows or darts. The general appearance of the upper parts of the plumage is glossy olive brown; some of the feathers quite plain, others spotted on the edges with dark brown, and those on the shoulders, scapulars, and tertials transversely marked with the same coloured waved bars, on a pale rusty ground: bastard wing and primary quills dark brown; inner webs of the latter deeply edged with white, freckled with brown, and some of those quills next the secondaries elegantly marked, near their tips, with narrow brown lines, pointed and shaped to the form of each feather: some of the secondaries are barred in nearly the same manner, others are white: back white; tail feathers and coverts beautifully marked with alternate bars of dusky and white, the middle ones slightly tinged with rust colour: legs red, and measure from the end of the toes to the upper bare part of the thigh, four inches and a half.

This species is of a solitary character, being mostly seen alone, or in pairs only. It resides the greater part of the year in the fen countries, where it breeds and rears its young. It lays four eggs, whitish, tinged with olive, and marked with irregular spots of black, chiefly on the thicker end.

THE LAPWING

Pee-wit, Bastard Plover, or Te-wit

(Tringa vanellus, Linn.—Le Vanneau, Buff.)

Is about the size of a Pigeon. Bill black; eyes large and hazel; top of the head black, glossed with green; a tuft of long narrow feathers issues from the back part of the head, and turns upwards at the end; some of them four inches in length: sides of the head and neck white, interrupted by a black streak above and below the eye; back part of the neck very pale brown; fore part, and the breast, black; back and the wing coverts dark green, glossed with purple and blue; quills black, the first four tipped with white; breast and belly pure white; upper tail coverts and vent pale chestnut; tail white at the base, the rest of it black, with pale tips, outer feathers almost wholly white: legs red; claws black; hind claw very short.

This bird subsists chiefly on worms and is often seen in great numbers by the seashores, where it finds an abundant supply. It is well known by its loud and incessant cries, from which a name has been given to it, imitative of the sound. The Pee-wit is a lively, active bird, almost continually in motion; it sports and frolics in the air in all directions, and assumes a variety of attitudes; it remains long upon the wing, and sometimes rises to a considerable height; it runs along the ground very nimbly, and springs from spot to spot with great agility. The female lays four eggs, of a dirty olive, spotted with black: she makes no nest, but deposits them upon a little dry grass scraped together: the young run very soon after they are hatched: during this period the old ones are very assiduous in their attention; on the approach of any person they flutter round his head with cries of the greatest inquietude, which increase as he draws near the spot where the brood are squatted; in case of extremity, and as a last resource, they run along the ground as if lame, in order to draw off the attention of the fowler from any further pursuit. The young Lapwings acquire their beautiful plumage about the latter end of July. At this time they assemble in flocks, which hover in the air, saunter in the meadows, and after rain, disperse among the ploughed fields.

THE GREEN SANDPIPER

(Tringa Ochropus, Linn.—Le Becasseau, ou Cul-blanc, Buff.)

This bird measures about ten inches in length, to the end of the toes nearly twelve, and weighs about three ounces and a half. The bill is black, and an inch and a half long: a pale streak extends from it over each eye; between which and the corners of the mouth, there is a dusky patch. The crown of the head and hinder part of the neck are dingy brownish ash, in some narrowly streaked with white: throat white: fore part of the neck mottled or streaked with brown spots, on a white or pale ash ground. The whole upper parts of the plumage glossy bronze, or olive brown, elegantly marked on the edge of each feather with small roundish white spots: the quills are without spots, and of a darker brown: the secondaries and tertials very long: insides of the wings dusky, edged with white grey; inside coverts next the body curiously barred, from the shaft of each feather to the edge, with narrow white lines, formed nearly of the shape of two sides of a triangle. Belly, vent, tail coverts, and tail, white; the last broadly barred with black, the middle feathers having four bars, and those next to them decreasing the number of bars towards the outside feathers, which are quite plain: legs green.

This bird is not anywhere numerous, and is of a solitary disposition, seldom more than a pair being seen together, and that chiefly in the breeding season. It is scarce in England, but is said to be more common in the northern parts of the globe, even as far as Iceland. It is reported that they never frequent the seashores, but their places of abode are commonly on the margins of lakes in the interior and mountainous parts of the country.

THE KNOT

Knute, or Knout

(*Tringa Canutus*, Linn.—*Le Canut*, Buff.)

These birds, which seem to be a connecting link between the Solopax and Tringa genera, differ considerably from each other in their appearance, in different seasons of the year, as well as from age and sex. The specimen from which the above drawing was taken, measured from the point of the bill to the tip of the tail, eight inches and a half, the extended wings about fifteen, and it weighed two ounces eight drachms: bill one inch three eighths long, black at the tip, and dusky, fading into orange towards the base; tongue of nearly the same length, sharp and horny at the point; sides of the head, neck, and breast, cinereous, edged with ash grey; chin white, and a stroke of the same passed over each eye. All upper parts of the plumage darkish brown, but more deep and glossy on the crown of the head, back and scapulars, and each feather edged with ash or grey; under parts cream coloured white, streaked or spotted with brown on the sides and vent; greater coverts of the wings tipped with white, forming a bar across them when extended: legs reddish yellow, and short, not measuring more than two inches and one eighth from the middle toe nail to the knee: thighs feathered very nearly to the knees; toes divided without any connecting membrane.

These birds are caught in Lincolnshire and the other fenny counties, in great numbers,[1] by nets, into which it is decoyed by carved wooden figures, painted to represent itself, and placed within them, much in the same way as the Ruff. It is also fattened for sale, and esteemed by many equal to the Ruff in the delicacy of its flavour. The season for taking it is from August to November.

This bird is said to have been a favourite dish with Canute, king of England; and Camden observes, that its name is derived from his – Knute, or Knout, as he was called, which, in process of time, has been changed to Knot.

1 *Pennant says fourteen dozen have been taken at once. [Bewick's note.]*

THE COMMON SANDPIPER

(Tringa hypoleucos, Linn.—*La Guignette,* Buff.*)*

This bird weighs about two ounces, and measures seven inches and a half in length. The bill is about an inch long, black at the tip, fading into pale brown towards the base. The head and hinder part of the neck are brownish ash, streaked downwards with dark narrow lines: the throat is white, and a streak of the same colour surrounds and is extended over each eye: the cheeks and auriculars are streaked with brown: the fore part of the neck to the breast is white, mottled and streaked with spots and lines of brown, pointing downwards: in some the breast is plain white: belly and vent white. The ground colour of all the upper parts of the plumage is ash, blended with glossy olive bronze brown: the coverts, scapulars, lower part of the back and tail coverts, are edged with dull white, and most elegantly marked with transverse dark narrow waved lines: the first two quills are plain brown; the next nine are marked on the middle of their inner webs, with white spots; the secondaries are also marked in the same manner, on both webs, and tipped with white. The tail consists of twelve feathers: the four middle ones olive brown, dark at the tips; those next, on each side, are much lighter coloured, mottled with dark brown, and tipped with white; the two outside ones are edged and tipped in the same manner, but are barred on their webs with dark brown: legs pale dull green, faintly blushed with red.

This elegant bird breeds in this country, but is not numerous; yet they are frequently seen in pairs during the summer months; and are well known by their clear piping note, by their flight, by jerking up their tails, and by their manner of running after their insect prey on the pebbly margins of brooks and rivers. The female makes her nest in a hole on the ground near their haunts; her eggs, commonly five in number, are mottled and marked with dark spots, on a yellowish ground. They leave England in the autumn, but whither they go is not particularly noticed.

153

THE RED-LEGGED SANDPIPER

(Tringa Bewickii, Montagu.)

This bird measures from the tip of the beak to the end of the tail, ten inches. The bill is an inch and three eighths long, black at the tip, and reddish towards the base: crown of the head spotted with dark brown, disposed in streaks, and edged with pale brown and grey: a darkish patch covers the space between the corners of the mouth and the eyes: chin white: brow and cheeks pale brown, grey and ash, with a few indistinct dusky spots; fore part, and breast white, clouded with a dull cinnamon colour, and sparingly and irregularly marked with black spots, reflecting a purple gloss: shoulder and scapular feathers black, edged with pale rust, and having the same glossy reflections as those on the breast: tertials nearly of the same length as the quills, and marked like the first annexed figure: ridges of the wings brownish ash; coverts, back, and rump nearly the same, but inclining to olive, and the middle of each feather of a deeper dusky brown: primary quills deep olive brown: exterior webs of the secondaries also of

that colour, but lighter, edged and tipped with white, and the inner webs are mostly white towards the base: tail coverts glossy black, edged with pale rust, and tipped with white; but in some of them a streak of white passes from the middle upwards, nearly the whole length, as in the second figure. The tail feathers are lightish brown, except the two middle ones, which are barred with large spots of a darker hue: the belly and vent white: legs bare above the knees, and red as sealing wax; claws black. The female is less than the male, and her plumage more dingy and indistinct: an egg taken out of her previous to stuffing, was surprisingly large, considering her bulk, being about the size of that of a Magpie, of a greenish white colour, spotted and blotched with brown, of a long shape, and pointed at the smaller end.

The foregoing figure and description were taken from a pair which were shot on Rippengale fen, in Lincolnshire, on the 14th of May, 1799, by Major Charles Dilke, of the Warwickshire cavalry.

THE DUNLIN

(Tringa Alpina, Linn.—*La Brunette*, Buff.)

Is nearly the size of the Judcock, and its bill is of the same shape, but much shorter in proportion to the bulk: it may also be easily distinguised among its associates, the Purres, Dotterels, Sanderlings, &c. by the redness of the upper parts of its plumage; the ground colour of which, from the beak to the rump, is ferruginous, or rusty red; but the middle of each feather is black, and the edges of some of them narrowly fringed with yellowish white, or ash grey; in some specimens the lesser wing coverts are dingy ash brown; in others clear brown, edged with ferruginous brown, the latter deeply tipped with white, which, together with the bases of the secondaries, forms an oblique bar across the extended wings: the primaries, except the first three, are edged on the exterior webs with white; shafts also mostly white, and each feather is sharply pencilled and distinctly defined with a light colour about the tips: a darkish spot covers each side of the head from the corners of the mouth, and a pale streak passes from the bill over each eye: the throat and fore part of the neck to the breast, are yellowish white, mottled with brown spots: a dusky crescent-shaped patch, the feathers of which are narrowly edged with white, covers the breast, the horns pointing towards the thighs:[1] the belly and vent are white: the middle tail feathers black, edged with ferruginous; the others pale ash, edged with white; legs and thighs black. The female is rather larger than the male, but in other respects resembles him pretty nearly.

The above description and figure were taken from a pair, sent by the Rev. C. Rudston, of Sandbutton, near York, the 22nd of April, 1799; and the author has been favoured with numbers of these and others of the same genus, by the Rev. H. Cotes, vicar of Bedlington; not two of which were exactly alike, probably owing to the difference of age or sex.

1 *In some specimens, supposed to be female, this patch was wanting.*
 [Bewick's note.]

THE LITTLE STINT
Little Sandpiper, or Least Snipe
(Tringa pusilla, Linn.—*La petite Alouette de Mer,* Brisson.*)*

This bird, the least of the Sandpiper tribe, nearly resembles the last species. It weighs twelve penny-weights troy; length nearly six inches; breadth rather more than eleven; the bill, to the corners of the mouth, is five eighths of an inch. The feathers on the crown of the head are black, edged with rusty: it is marked, like most of the genus, by a light streak over each eye, and a dark spot below and before them: the throat, fore part of the neck, and belly are white; and the breast is tinged with pale reddish yellow: the shoulders and scapulars black, edged with white on the exterior webs of each feather, and on the interior with rust: back and tail dusky: legs slender, and nearly black.

1 *Our bird was shot by Robert Pearson, Esq. of Newcastle, on the 10th of September, 1801. [Bewick's note.]*

156

THE TURNSTONE

Sea Dotterel, or Hebridal Sandpiper

(Tringa interpres, Linn.—*Le Coulon-chaud*, Buff.*)*

This is a plump-made, and prettily variegated bird, and measures about eight inches and a quarter in length. The bill is black, straight, strong, and not more than an inch in length: the ground colour of the head and neck white, with small spots on the crown and hinder parts; a black stroke crosses the forehead to the eyes: the auriculars are formed by a patch of the same colour, which, pointing forward to the corners of the mouth, and falling down, is spread over the sides of the breast, whence ascends another branch, which, like a band, goes about the lower part of the neck behind.[1] The back, scapulars, and tertials are black, edged with rusty red: lesser coverts of the wings cinereous brown; greater coverts black, edged with ferruginous, and tipped with white: primary and secondary quills black, the latter white at the ends: rump and tail coverts white, crossed with a black bar: tail black, tipped with white: fore part of the breast, belly and vent white: thighs feathered nearly to the knees: legs and feet red. This and the succeeding bird are now said to be the same species, and differing only from age or sex. It is quite obvious that it ought to be separated from the genus *Tringa*, to which it bears little affinity. Temminck has done so, and formed it into a new genus (*Strepsilas*).

1 *In some specimens the lower part of the neck is white. [Bewick's note.]*

157

THE OYSTER-CATCHER

Pied Oyster-catcher, Sea-pie, or Olive
(*Hæmatopus Ostralegus*, Linn.—*L'Huîtrier*, Buff.)

The Oyster-catcher generally weighs about sixteen ounces, measures seventeen inches in length, and two feet eight inches in breadth. The bill is bright scarlet, about three inches long, wide at the nostrils, and grooved beyond them nearly half its length; thence to the tip it is vertically compressed on the sides, and in old birds ends obtusely: with this instrument, which, in its shape and structure, is peculiar to this bird, it easily disengages the limpets from the rocks, and is said to pluck out the oysters from their half-opened shells: on these it feeds, as well as on other kinds of shellfish, sea-worms, and insects. The irides are lake red; orbits orange; under orbit white, and (in many specimens) a crescent-shaped stroke of this colour crosses the throat; head, neck, upper part of the back, scapulars, lesser coverts of the wings and the end of the tail black; quills, in some, dark brown, striped less or more in the middle and inner webs with white: secondary quills white towards their base, the uncovered points black, narrowly edged with white; breast, belly, upper half of the tail, lower part of the back and greater wing coverts white: legs and feet pale red; the toes, three in number, are short and strong, each surrounded with a membraneous edge, and covered with a hard scaly skin, which enables the bird to traverse and climb the rough and sharp shell-covered rocks, in quest of prey, without injury.

Although the Oyster-catcher is not provided with powers fitted for an expert swimmer, yet it does not show any aversion to taking the water, upon which it may be said to float rather than swim. When wounded and pursued, it can dive with great quickness, and remain a considerable time underwater. These birds are the constant inhabitants of the seashores, and are seldom found inland. In winter they assemble in flocks, are then shy and wild, and are seen in pairs only in the breeding season and in the summer.

THE AVOSET
Scooper, Crooked-bill, or Yelper
(*Recurvirostra Avosetta*, Linn.—*L'Avocette*, Buff.)

This bird, which is the only European species of Avoset, does not much exceed the Lapwing in the bulk of its body; but, from the length of its legs, it is much taller.

It measures about eighteen inches in length, to the end of the toes twenty-two, from tip to tip thirty, and weighs from twelve to fourteen ounces. The bill is black, about three inches and a half long, and of a singular conformation, looking not unlike flexible flat pieces of whalebone, curved upwards to the tip: irides hazel: head round, black on the upper part to below the nape of the neck: above and beneath each eye, in most specimens, there are small white spots; but in the one from which the above figure was taken, a streak of that colour passed over each eye towards the hinder part of the head. The thighs are naked, and, as well as the legs and feet, are of a fine pale blue. The whole plumage of the Avoset is white, intersected with black; and, like most of the variegated or piebald birds, the patches of these colours are not placed exactly the same in every individual; therefore, as the bird cannot be mistaken, a more minute description is unnecessary.

These birds are common in the winter about the lakes, mouths of rivers, and marshes, in the southern parts of England; and assemble in large flocks on the fens, in the breeding season. When the female is frightened off her nest, she counterfeits lameness; and when a flock is disturbed, they fly with their necks stretched out, and their legs extended behind them, over the head of the spectator, much in the same way as the Lapwing or Peewit, making a shrill noise, and uttering a yelping cry of *twit, twit,* all the time. The places where they have been feeding may be traced out by the semi-circular marks left in the mud or sand by their bills in scooping out their food, which consists of spawn, worms, insects, &c.

THE KINGFISHER

(Alcedo ispida, Linn.—*Le Martin-pêcheur*, Buff.)

This splendid little bird is of rather a clumsy shape, the head being large in proportion to the size of the body, and the legs and feet very small. The length is only seven inches, breadth eleven; weight about two ounces and a quarter. The bill, measured from the corners of the mouth, is two inches long, vertically compressed on the sides, strong, straight, and tapering to a sharp point: the upper mandible is black, fading into red towards the base; the under one, as well as the inside of the mouth, reddish orange: irides hazel, inclining to red. A broad stripe passes from the bill over the eye to the hinder part of the neck, of a bright orange, but margined on the side of the mouth, and crossed below the eye, by a narrow black stroke, and terminated behind the auriculars with a slanting wedge-shaped white spot. The throat is white; the head, and the wing coverts are a deep shining green, spotted with bright light blue: the scapulars and exterior webs of the quills are of the same colour, but without spots. The middle of the back, the rump, and coverts of the tail are of a most resplendent azure: the tail, which consists of twelve short feathers, is deep rich blue, and the whole under part of the body, bright orange. The legs and toes are red, and are peculiar in their shape and conformation, the three forward toes being unconnected from the claws to the first joints, from whence they appear as if grown into each other; and the inner and hinder ones are placed in a line on the inside of the foot, whereby the heel is widened, and seems pressed out.

It is difficult to conceive why ornithologists have classed the Kingfisher with land birds, as its habits and manner of living are wholly confined to the fresh waters, on the margins of which it will sit for hours together on a projecting twig, or stone; at one while fluttering its wings, and exposing its brilliant plumage to the sun; at another, hovering in the air like the Kestrel, it waits the moment when it may seize its prey, on which it darts almost unerringly: often it remains for several seconds under the water, before it has gained the object of its pursuit, then brings up the little fish, which it carries to the land, beats to death, and swallows.

The female commonly makes her nest by the sides of rivers or brooks, in a hole made by the mole, or the water-rat: this she enlarges or contracts to suit her purpose; and it is conjectured, from the difficulty of finding the nest, that frequently the hole which leads to it is underwater. The eggs are clear white.

To notice the many strange and contradictory accounts of this bird, as well as of its nest, transmitted to us by the ancients,[1] and to enumerate the properties ascribed to it by the superstitious in all ages, would occupy too large a portion of this work: but the following modern instance seems worthy of notice:—

Dr Heysham, of Carlisle, in his *Catalogue of Cumberland Animals*, says, 'On the 7th of May a boy from Upperby brought me a Kingfisher alive, which he had taken when sitting on her eggs the night before: from him I received the following information:—Having often this spring observed these birds frequent a bank upon the river Peteril, he watched them carefully, and saw them go into a small hole in the bank. The hole was too small to admit his hand, but as it was made in the soft mould, he

easily enlarged it. It was upwards of half a yard long; at the end of it the eggs, which were six in number, were placed upon the bare mould, there being not the smallest appearance of a nest.'

Kingfishers are not so numerous as might be expected from the number of eggs found in their nests, owing probably to the young being destroyed by the floods, which must often rise above the level of the holes where they are bred.

Except in the breeding season, this bird is usually seen alone, flying near the surface of the water with the rapidity of an arrow, like a little brilliant meteor, by which appearance the eye is enabled to follow its long-continued course. Considering the shortness of its wings, the velocity with which it flies is surprising.

Ornithologists inform us that Kingfishers are found in almost every part of the globe; but it does not appear that more than this one species has ever been seen in Europe.

---

1 *Their nests are wonderful – of the figure of a ball rather elevated, with a very narrow mouth; they look like a large sponge: they cannot be cut with a knife, but may be broken with a smart stroke: they have the appearance of petrified sea-froth. It is not discovered of what they are formed; some think of Prickly-back bones, since they live upon fish.—Pliny.*

Aristotle compares the nest to a gourd, and its substance and texture to those sea-balls or lumps of interwoven filaments which are cut with difficulty; but, when dried, become friable.

Ælian and Plutarch describe it as being made to float on the placid face of the ocean. [Bewick's note.]

THE WATER RAIL

Bilcock, Velvet Runner, or Brook Ouzel

(Rallus aquaticus, Linn.—*Le Rale d'Eau*, Buff.*)*

This bird, though a distinct genus of itself, has many traits in its character very similar to both the Land Rail and the Spotted Rail: it is migratory, like the former, to which it also bears resemblance in size, and shape; its haunts and manner of living are nearly the same as those of the latter; but it differs from both in the length of its bill, and in its plumage. It weighs about four ounces and a half, and measures twelve inches in length and sixteen in breadth. The bill is slightly curved, and one inch and three quarters long; the upper mandible dusky, edged with red; the under reddish orange; irides red. The top of the head, hinder part of the neck, the back, scapulars, coverts of the wings, and tail, are black, edged dingy brown; the ridge of the wings is white, the bastard wing barred with white, the inside barred with brown and white, and the quills and secondaries dusky; the side feathers are beautifully crossed with black and white, and slightly tipped with pale reddish brown. The inner side of the thighs, the belly, and the vent are pale brown, and in some specimens, speckled with bluish ash. The sides of the head, the chin, fore part of the neck, and the breast, are dark hoary lead colour, slightly tinged with pale rufous. The tail consists of twelve short black feathers, edged and tipped with dirty red; some on the under side barred with black and white. The legs, which are placed far behind, are a dull red; toes long, without any connecting membrane. The eggs are more than an inch and a half long, pale yellowish, marked all over with dusky brown spots.

The Water Rail is a shy and solitary bird. Its constant abode is in low wet places, much overgrown with sedges, reeds, and other coarse herbage, among which it shelters and feeds in hidden security. It is not very common in Great Britain, but is numerous in the marshes of the northern countries of Europe, whence, partially and irregularly, it migrates southward into Africa, during the severity of the winter season.

THE LAND-RAIL, OR CORN-CRAKE

Darker Hen

(Gallinula Crex, Lath.—*Le Rale de Genet*, Buff.*)*

Length rather more than nine inches, body compressed. Bill light brown; eyes hazel; all the feathers on the upper parts of the plumage dark brown, edged with pale rust; both wing coverts and quills deep chestnut; fore part of the neck and the breast pale ash; a streak of the same colour extends over each eye from the bill to the side of the neck; belly yellowish white; sides, thighs, and vent marked with faint rusty-coloured bars: legs pale flesh red.

The Land-rail makes its appearance about the same time as the Quail, and frequents the same places. Its well-known cry is first heard as soon as the grass becomes long enough to shelter it, and continues till the grass is cut; but the bird is seldom seen, for it skulks among the thickest part of the herbage.

The Corn-crake leaves this island before the winter, and repairs to other countries in search of its food, which consists principally of slugs, of which it destroys prodigious numbers; it likewise feeds on shell snails, (*helix nemorallis*), worms and insects of various kinds, as well as on seeds. It has no craw, but a wide pipe descending direct to the gizzard. It is very common in Ireland, and is seen in great numbers in the island of Anglesea in its passage to that country. On its first arrival in England, it is so lean as to weigh less than six ounces, from which one would conclude that it must have come from distant parts; before its departure, however, it has been known to exceed eight ounces, and is then very delicious eating. The female lays ten or twelve eggs, on a nest made of a little moss or dry grass loosely put together: they are of a pale ash colour, marked with rust-coloured spots. The young Crakes are covered with a black down; they soon find the use of their legs, for they follow the mother immediately after they have burst the shell.

The foregoing figure was made from a living bird, for which the work is indebted to the late Major H. F. Gibson.

THE SPOTTED RAIL, OR SPOTTED GALLINULE

(Gallinula Porzana, Linn.—La Marouette, Buff.)

Weighs above four ounces, and measures nearly nine inches in length, and about fifteen in breadth. Bill greenish yellow, and not more than three quarters of an inch long. Top of the head to the nape dusky, slightly streaked with rusty brown; a brown and white mottled stripe passes from the bill over and behind the eyes; cheeks and throat freckled dull grey. Neck and breast olive, marked with small white spots; sides dusky and olive, crossed with bars of white, and the under parts are a mixture of cinereous dirty white and yellow. The plumage of all the upper parts is dusky and olive brown, spotted, edged, barred or streaked with white; spots on the wing coverts surrounded with black, giving a studded appearance; and the white bars and streaks on the scapulars and tertials form a beautiful contrast with the black ground of the feathers. The legs are yellowish green.

Its common abode is in low swampy grounds, in which are pools or streamlets, overgrown with willows, reeds, and rushes, where it lurks and hides itself: it is wild, solitary, and shy. The species is very scarce in Great Britain, and from its extreme vigilance rarely to be seen. It is supposed to be migratory here, as well as in France and Italy, where it is found early in the spring: it is met with in other parts of Europe, but nowhere in great numbers. Its nest is made of rushes and other light buoyant materials, woven and matted together, so as to float on, and to rise or fall with the ebbing or flowing of the water, like a boat; and to prevent its being swept away by floods, it is moored to the pendant stalk of one of the reeds, by which it is screened from sight, and sheltered from the weather. The female lays from six to eight eggs. The young brood do not long require the fostering care of the mother, but as soon as they are hatched, the whole of the little black shapeless family scramble away from her, take to the water, separate from each other, and shift for themselves.

THE COOT

(Fulica atra, Linn.—La Foulque, ou Morrelle, Buff.)

This bird generally weighs about twenty-eight ounces, and measures fifteen inches in length. The bill is greenish white, more than an inch and a quarter long: a white membrane, like that of the Water Hen, but larger, is spread over the forehead, which changes its colour to a pale red in the breeding season: irides red: the upper parts of its plumage black, except the outer edges of the wings, and a spot under each eye, which are white: under parts hoary dark ash or lead colour. The skin is clothed with a thick down, and covered with close fine feathers: thighs placed far behind, fleshy and strong, bare, and yellow above the knees: legs and toes commonly of a yellowish green, but sometimes of a lead colour.

The Coot has many features like the Rails and the Water Hens but it is a genus distinct from those birds, and from the waders in general, on account of its being fin-footed, and its constant attachment to the waters. It may be said not to walk, but to splash and waddle between one pool and another. These birds, like those of the preceding kinds, hide themselves, during the day, among rushes and weeds, which grow abundantly in the loughs and ponds where they take up their constant abode: they rarely venture abroad, except in the dusk, and in the night, in quest of their food, which consists of the herbage, seeds, insects, and the slippery inhabitants of stagnant waters.

This species is met with in Great Britain all year but removes in the autumn from the lesser pools where the young have been reared to larger lakes, where flocks assemble in the winter. They commonly build their nest in rushes, surrounded by water: it is composed of a great quantity of dried weeds, matted together, and lined within with softer and finer grasses: the female lays from twelve to fifteen eggs, and commonly hatches twice in a season; the eggs are about the size of those of a pullet, and are of a pale brownish white, sprinkled with small dark spots.

THE GREY PHALAROPE

Coot-footed Tringa, or Scallop-toed Sandpiper

(Phalaropus Lobatus, Lath.—*Le Phalarope à festons dentelés,* Buff.*)*

The bill is nearly an inch long: the upper mandible is dusky horn colour, grooved on each side, and flatted near the tip; the under one is orange towards the base. The eyes are placed high in the head, with a dark patch underneath each, and the same on the hinder part of the head and neck. The shoulder and scapular feathers are fine lead grey, edged with white: fore part of the head, throat, neck, and breast, white: belly also white, but slightly dashed with pale rust: greater coverts broadly tipped with white, which forms an oblique bar across the wings, when they are closed: some of the first and secondary quills are narrowly edged with white: on the middle of the back the feathers are brown, edged with bright rust: on the rump there are several feathers of the same colour, but mixed with others of white, rufous, and lemon. The wings are long, and, when closed, reach beyond the tail: the primary quills are dusky, the lower part of their inner sides white: secondaries tipped with white: tail dusky, edged with ash: legs black. The scalloped membranes on its toes (in our specimen) differed from those of the Red Phalarope, in being finely serrated on their edges.

This bird is a native of the northern regions of Europe, Asia, and America, and migrates southward in the winter. It has seldom been met with in any part of the British isles. Ray, however, saw one at Brignal, in Yorkshire; and Pennant mentions one which was shot in the same county; Mr Tunstall another, shot at Stavely, in Derbyshire;—and the specimen from which this drawing and description were taken, was shot near the city of Chester, by Lieutenant-Colonel Dalton, of the 4th regiment of Dragoons, on the 14th of October, 1800.

Capt. Sabine mentions in his *Memoir of the Birds of Greenland,* that on the 10th of June, in latitude 68°, four miles from land, a flock of these birds was seen swimming in the open sea amongst icebergs.

THE RED-NECKED PHALAROPE

(Phalaropus Fuscus, Lath.—*Le Phalarope Brun,* Brisson.)

Bill an inch long, flattened and black at the tip; rest of both mandibles orange coloured; head capped with dusky brown, extending from the bill to the hinder part; throat and about the corners of the mouth, also of the same colour, but paler and inclining to ash: cheeks and sides of the head white, which, meeting at the nape of the neck, gradually deepens into ash and dusky brown towards the shoulders; the latter, with the scapulars and tail coverts, are black, tipped, bordered, and striped with pale rusty yellow; middle of the back, and the lesser and greater coverts dusky ash, the latter tipped with white; tertials and the exterior webs of the quills dusky; but the greater part of the inner webs of the latter are pale ash, fading into white: the tail consists of twelve feathers; the two middle ones, which are the longest, are plain dusky brown; the rest taper off in length, and turn lighter coloured as they shorten, and are margined on the outer webs with pale rusty yellow and white; the whole of the under parts, from the throat to the end of the vent feathers, are deep reddish chestnut; legs and toes yellowish, and scalloped like those of the Grey Phalarope, but the middle claws, which are short, hooked, and sharp, are turned outward. The above description was taken from a male bird brought from Davis's Straits, where they are numerous about the mouth of Hudson's river. Although very fat and plump, they are extremely active, and swim about nimbly in quest of their food, which consists chiefly of the slimy substance called whale's food, so frequently seen floating on the surface of the waters of the northern seas. They are occasionally met with on the British shores.

The author was furnished by Mr Charles Fothergill, with two stuffed specimens, male and female, and the eggs of these birds. The above figure was taken from the former. It differs in its plumage from the red Phalarope; its head, and a narrow stripe on the front, another on the hinder part of the neck, which last spread over the shoulder, were dark ash; throat white; sides of the neck and breast brilliant bay colour; upper parts of the plumage deep brown, nearly black; under parts white. The eggs, four in number, like those of others of this genus, were large; they were of a dingy olive, blotched and spotted with brown.

167

THE GREAT-CRESTED GREBE

Greater-crested Doucker, Cargoose, Ash-coloured Loon, or Gaunt

(Podiceps cristatus, Lath.—Le Grêbe cornu, Buff.)

This is the largest of the Grebes, weighing about two pounds and a half, and measuring twenty-one inches in length, and thirty in breadth. The bill is about two inches and a quarter long, dark at the tip, and red at the base: the bare stripe between the bill and the eyes, is, in the breeding season, red, but afterwards changes to dusky: irides, fine pale crimson. The head is furnished with a great quantity of feathers, which form a kind of ruff, surrounding the upper part of the neck; those on each side of the head, behind, are longer and stand out like ears: this ruff is of a bright ferruginous colour, edged on the under side with black. The upper parts of the plumage are of a sooty or mouse-coloured brown; under parts glossy or silvery white; the inner ridge of the wing is white; the secondaries the same, forming an oblique bar across the wings, when closed: the outside of the legs is dusky, the inside and toes pale green.

This species is common in the fens and lakes in various parts of England. The female conceals her nest among the flags and reeds which grow in the water, upon which it is said to float, and that she hatches her eggs amidst the moisture which oozes through it. It is made of various kinds of dried fibres, stalks and leaves of water plants; when it happens to be blown from the reeds, it floats upon the surface of the open water.

These birds are met with in almost every lake in the northern parts of Europe, as far as Iceland, and southward to the Mediterranean; they are also found in various parts of America.

THE DUSKY GREBE

Black and White Dobchick

(Podiceps obscurus, Lath.—*Le petit Grêbe,* Buff.

Measures about an inch less in length, and two in breadth, than the last. The bill is more than an inch long, pale blue, with reddish edges: lore and orbits red: irides bright yellow, without that red; upper part of the head, hinder part of the neck, scapulars, and rump, dark sooty, or mouse-coloured brown: feathers on the back nearly of the same colour, but glossy, and with greyish edges: ridge of the wings and secondary quills white; the rest of the wing dusky. There is a pale spot before each eye; cheeks and throat white: fore part of the neck light brown; and the breast and belly white and glossy, like satin: thighs and vent covered with dirty white downy feathers: legs white behind, dusky on the outer sides, and pale blue on the inner sides and shins: the toes and webbed membranes are also blue on the upper sides, and dark underneath.

This description was taken from a very perfect bird, caught on Sand Hutton Car, near York, on the 28th of January, 1799, by the Rev. C. Rudston: other specimens of this species have differed in the shades of their plumage and colour of the bill: in some the upper mandible is yellow, from the nostrils to the corners of the mouth, and the under one entirely of that colour.

THE BLACK GUILLEMOT

Greenland Dove, Sea Turtle, or Tyste

(Uria Grylle, Lath.—Le petit Guillemot noir, Buff.)

Length about fourteen inches, breadth twenty-two, weight fourteen ounces. Bill black, slender shaped, and pointed; the upper mandible slightly bent at the point: inside of the mouth red. The whole plumage is sleek and glossy, and of a sooty-coloured black, excepting a large patch of white on the coverts of each wing: its feathers appear all unwebbed, and look like silky hair: legs and feet red: claws black. In some the whole plumage is black; in others the lesser quills are tipped with white; and all those that remain in the northern climates are said to turn white in winter.

These birds are met with in the North Sea, in Greenland, Spitzbergen, Iceland, the Faroe, Orkney, and Shetland Islands; in the latter they are known to breed in considerable numbers. The nest is made in the deep crevices of the rocks which overhang the sea: the eggs are of a grey colour: some assert that the female lays only one, and others with more probability, that she lays two. They commonly fly in pairs, and so low that on being flushed they raise the surface of the sea by the flapping of their narrow wings. This is a sprightly active bird.

The Greenlanders eat the flesh, and use its skin for clothing and the legs as a bait for their fishing lines. Willoughby, Ray, Albin, and Edwards have named it the Greenland Dove, or Sea Turtle. In the Orkney Islands it is called the Tyste or Puffinet.

The foregoing figure was taken from a drawing presented to the author.

THE GREAT NORTHERN DIVER

Loon, Imbrim, or Embergoose

(Colymbus glacialis, Linn.*—L'Imbrim,* Buff.*)*

The Great Diver weighs about sixteen pounds; measures three feet six inches in length, and four feet eight in breadth. The bill is black, four inches and a half long, and strongly formed: the head is of a deep black, glossed with green and purple reflections: the neck appears as if wrapped obliquely round with a bandage of the same colours as the head; the feathers in the spaces between are white, streaked down the middle with narrow black lines; the sides of the breast are marked in the same manner: the whole of the upper parts are black, spotted with white: the spots on the scapulars are the largest, and of an oblong square shape, placed in rows, two on the end of each feather: the under parts are white: quills and tail black. The female is less than the male, and her whole upper plumage inclines more to brown. Her under parts are of a dirty white, and the bandages on her neck, and the spots on her body are not so distinct.

This species seldom visits the British shores, except in very severe winters. One was shot on the Tyne, at Newcastle, on the 12th October, 1824, supposed to have been driven from its northern haunts by the severe storm, from the north-east, which then raged for two days, on this coast. In the summer season it inhabits the north of Europe, and the arctic coasts, as far as the river Ob in the Russian dominions, and Hudson's Bay, in North America. They seldom quit the sea, or are seen inland, except at the breeding season, when they repair to the freshwater lakes in the Faroe Isles, Spitzbergen, Iceland, Greenland, and Shetland, &c. The female lays only two eggs, which are of a dirty white or stone colour: when she quits her nest, she flies very high, and on her return darts down upon it in an oblique direction.

THE COMMON TERN

Great Tern, Kirmew, or Sea-swallow

(Sterna Hirundo, Linn.—La grande Hirondelle de Mer, Buff.)

Measures above fourteen inches in length, thirty in breadth, and weighs more than four ounces. The bill is crimson, tipped with black, and about two inches and a quarter in length: the head is capped with a longish black patch, which extends over the eyes, and ends in a point below the nape of the neck: the throat, cheeks, neck, and the whole of the under parts are white: the tail, which is long, and greatly forked, is also white, except the two outside feathers, which are black on their exterior webs; but in flying, this fork is frequently closed so as to look like a single feather. The upper part of the plumage is of a fine pale lead colour: the quills are of a deeper cast, the outside ones the darkest: the legs and feet red.

The female forms her nest in the moss or long coarse grass, near the lake, and lays three or four eggs of a dull olive, marked with different-sized black spots at the thicker end: it is said she covers them only during the night, or in the day when it rains; at all other times she leaves the hatching of them to the heat of the sun.

This clean-looking pretty bird is common in the summer months on the sea-coasts, rivers, and lakes of the British Isles, and is also met with in various parts of Europe, Asia, and America. It migrates southward to the Mediterranean, and to the Madeira and Canary Isles, and northward as far as Spitzbergen and Greenland.

THE LESSER TERN

Lesser Sea-swallow

(Sterna minuta, Linn.*—La petite Hirondelle de Mer,* Buff.*)*

Measures about eight inches in length, and nineteen in breadth, and weighs a little more than two ounces. It looks like the former species in miniature; is equally, if not more delicately elegant in its plumage and general appearance, and its manners and habits are much the same; but it is not nearly so numerous, or so widely dispersed. It differs from the Common Tern in having the black patch on its head divided by a white line on the front of the brow, and over each eye, in the tail being wholly white, and, in proportion to the size of the bird, much shorter or less forked, and in the bill and the feet being more inclined to orange or yellow. Nothing can exceed the clean, clear, and glossy whiteness of its close-set feathers on the under parts of the body; but the upper plumage is of a plain sober lead-coloured grey. The egg is an inch and a half in length, of a dirty yellowish brown, dashed all over with reddish blotches.

This bird is met with in the summer months on all our coasts, also about the Baltic, in some parts of Russia, the river Irtish in Siberia, the Black and Caspian Seas, and in America near New York, &c. In Belon's time 'the fishermen floated a cross of wood, in the middle of which was fastened a small fish for bait, with limed twigs stuck to the four corners, on which the bird darting, was entangled by the wings.'

THE SANDWICH TERN

(Sterna Cantiaca, Gm. Linn.)

A pair of these birds, male and female, was shot on the Farn Islands, on the coast of Northumberland, in July, 1802, from the former of which this figure was taken. They measured two feet nine inches from tip to tip of the wings: the bills were tipped with yellow: the black feathers which capped and adorned their heads were elongated behind, forming a kind of peaked crest, which overhung the nape and hinder part of the neck: the feathers of the fore part of the neck and breast, when ruffled up, appeared delicately and faintly blushed with red. In other respects they corresponded so nearly with Mr Latham's accurate description, that to attempt giving any other is needless.—'Length eighteen inches: bill two inches; colour black, with the tip horn colour: tongue half the length of the bill: irides hazel: fore-head, crown, hind head, and sides above the eyes black: the rest of the head, neck, under parts of the body and tail, white; the back and wings pale hoary lead colour: the first five quills hoary black, the inner webs deeply margined with white; the sixth like the others, but much paler: the rest of the quills like the back: the tail is forked, the outer feathers six inches and a quarter in length; the wings reach beyond it: legs and claws black: the under part of the feet dusky red. Some specimens have the top of the head dotted with white. In young birds the upper parts are much clouded with brown; and the whole of the top of the head greatly mixed with white: but this is not peculiar, as the young of other Terns with black heads are in the same state. It is pretty common on the Suffolk and Kentish coasts in the summer months, breeds there in the month of June, is supposed to lay its eggs upon the rocks, and to hatch them about the middle of July.' He adds, 'Whether these birds only visit us at uncertain seasons, or have hitherto passed unnoticed among other Terns, we know not; but believe that this has not yet been recorded as a British species.'

THE BLACK TERN

(Sterna fissipes, Linn.—*L'Epouvantail,* Buff.*)*

This bird generally measures ten inches in length, and twenty-four in breadth, and weighs about two ounces and a half. The bill is black, and from the tip to the brow is about an inch and a quarter long; the head, neck, breast, and under part, as far as the thighs, black; the lower belly and vent pale ash; the upper parts of the plumage, including the wings and tail, are dark hoary lead coloured blue; the tail is not greatly forked, nor long, and in most specimens, the exterior webs of the two outside feathers are white; the legs and feet crimson; claws black; the female does not differ materially in her appearance from the male.

This species frequents the sea shores in summer, but in habits and manners it differs somewhat from the rest of the Terns, with whom it does not associate.

The cry is shriller, and its evolutions and turnings while on the wing, shorter and more rapid. It seems to prefer the rivers, fens, marshes, and lakes, to the sea. The nest is built among reeds and rushes, in marshy places, with flags and coarse grass, upon a tuft just above the surface of the water. The eggs, four in number, are of a dirty greenish colour, spotted, and encircled with black about the thicker end. It feeds on beetles, maggots, and other insects, as well as on small fishes. Voyagers say it is met with at Hudson's Bay, Newfoundland, and Iceland, and that it is common in Siberia, and the salt lakes in the deserts of Tartary. Our figure was drawn from a preserved specimen in the Museum of Ravensworth Castle.

THE BLACK-BACKED GULL

Great Black and White Gull

(Larus marinus, Linn.—*Le Goéland noir manteau*, Buff.)

This species measures from twenty-six to twenty-nine inches in length, and five feet nine inches in breadth, and weighs nearly five pounds. The bill is pale yellow, very firm, strong, and thick, and nearly four inches long from the tip to the corners of the mouth: the projecting angle on the lower mandible is red, or orange, with a black spot in the middle, on each side: the irides are yellow, and the edges of the eyelids orange. The upper part of the back and wings black: all the other parts and the tips of the quills are white: legs pale flesh colour.

The Black-backed Gull is common in the northern parts of Europe, the rocky isles of the North Sea, and in Greenland. Though it was known to Fabricius, it must be very rare in the higher parts of Baffin's Bay, Captain Sabine having seen only one specimen there. They are only thinly scattered on the coasts of England, where they, however, sometimes remain to breed on the highest cliffs which overhang the sea. In their native haunts, their favorite breeding places are high inaccessible islets, covered with long coarse tufty grass. Their eggs are of a round shape, of a dark olive, thinly marked with dusky spots, and quite black at the thicker end. Their cry of *kac, kac, kac*, quickly repeated, is roughly hoarse and disagreeable.

1 *A curious habit of this bird is its constantly accompanying flocks of the Shag (Pelecanus Graculus) at those times of the day when they resort to their favorite rocks to rest themselves, or bask in the sun. Before the sportsman can approach within gunshot, their friendly sentinel, the Black-backed Gull, flies off, and with him all the Shags, excepting a few of the more stupid or very young birds, which not benefiting by the signal, generally fall a sacrifice. (Vide Dr Edmonston's View of the Shetland Islands.) [Bewick's note.]*

THE LESSER BLACK-BACKED GULL

(Larus fuscus, Linn.—*Le Goéland gris*, Briss.)

Is similar in appearance to the Black-backed Gull, but is much less, and is not quite so dark on the back as that bird is described to be. In the stuffed specimen presented to this work by Mr Laurence Edmondston, the upper plumage is of a dark bluish lead colour; the greater coverts, scapulars, and secondaries the same, but tipped with white; the primary quills, which are, in all the visible parts, of a dark brown, are also tipped with white; the rest of the plumage white; eyelids red; irides pale yellow; the bill the same, but of a much deeper tinge, and the angular knob of the under mandible is reddish orange: legs yellow.

Temminck says, 'It frequents the sea coasts in winter, and is met with migratory on the rivers and inland seas of the eastern parts of Europe. It is common in the Baltic; and in autumn is seen on its passage along the coasts of Holland and France, but more especially of the Mediterranean. It is likewise found in North America.' In this country, though pretty generally dispersed, it is nowhere numerous. Its mode and place of breeding are as yet but imperfectly known.

THE HERRING GULL

Silvery Gull

(Larus argentatus, Linn. (Gm.)—*Le Goéland à manteau gris ou cendré,* Buff.*)*

The weight of this bird exceeds thirty ounces; the length is about twenty-three inches, and the breadth fifty-two. The spot on the angular knob of the under mandible is deep orange; the rest of the bill yellow: irides pale yellow; edges of the eyelids red. The back and wing coverts are dark bluish ash: the first five quills in most specimens are black on the upper parts, and have each a roundish white spot on the outer webs near the tips; others are marked differently on the quills: legs pale flesh colour. The back and wings of some of this species, which are supposed to be the young not arrived at full plumage, are ash-coloured, spotted with brown.

The haunts, manners, and habits, as well as the general appearance of this Gull, are very similar to those of the preceding species, but this is much more common on the British shores: they make their nests of dry grass on the projecting ledges of the rocks, and lay three eggs of a dull white, spotted with black. They have obtained their name from pursuing and preying upon the shoals of herrings. Fishermen describe them as the constant, bold, intruding attendants on their nets, from which they find it difficult to drive them away. This species, like the preceding, is met with in the northern seas, but has been observed to wander farther into southern climates.

This Gull is remarkable by its habit of keeping watch over the safety of all birds, and even of seals, within the reach of its warnings. Upon the approach of the sportsman with his gun, it seems all upon the alert, and by its clamorous well known cries intimates their danger.

THE COMMON GULL

Common Sea Mall, or Mew

(Larus canus, Linn.*—La Grande Mouette cendrée,* Buff.*)*

The Common Gull generally measures between sixteen and seventeen inches in length, thirty-six, and sometimes more in breadth, and weighs about one pound. The bill is pale yellow, tinged with green, and an inch and three quarters long; irides hazel: edges of the eyelids red: the upper part of the head and cheeks, and the hinder part and sides of the neck are streaked with dusky spots: the back, scapulars, and wings are fine pale bluish grey: the throat, rump, tail, and all the under parts are pure white: the first two quills black, with a pretty large white spot near the tips; next four tipped with black, and the secondaries largely with white: legs greenish, or a dirty white. This is nearly the description of an individual; but from the number which the author has examined, it is certain that these birds vary, probably from age, climate, or season, in the markings of the head, quills, tail, and in the colour of the bills and feet, hardly two being found exactly alike. Some have the head quite white; some the quills plain black at the ends; others the tail tipped with black, and the feet blushed with red, green, or blue. Their plumage and look altogether is very clean and agreeable.

The habits and manners of this species are much the same as those of the rest of the genus: they are spread all over the globe, and are the most common and numerous of all the Gulls which frequent the British shores. They breed on the rocky cliffs; and lay two eggs, nearly of the size of those of a Hen, of an olive brown, marked with dark reddish blotches, or irregular spots. At the mouths of the larger rivers, they are seen in numbers, picking up the animal substances which are cast on shore, or come floating down with the tide: for this kind of food they watch with a quick eye, and it is curious to observe how such as are near the breakers will mount upon the surface of the water, and run splashing towards the summit of the wave to catch the object of their pursuit. They also, at particular seasons, resort to the inland parts to feed upon worms.

THE KITTIWAKE

Annett, or Tarrock

(*Larus tridactylus*,[1] Linn.—*Mouette cendrée tachetée ou Kutgechef*, Buff.)

Measures from fourteen to seventeen inches in length, thirty-eight to forty in breadth, and weighs generally about fourteen ounces. The bill is greenish yellow, the upper mandible more regularly arched than in any of the other species: the inside of the mouth and edges of the eyelids are orange: the irides dark: the head, neck, under parts and tail, pure white: back and wings lead or ash grey: the exterior edge of the first quill feather, and the tips of the next four or five are black: legs dusky: hinder toe not bigger than a small wart. Some specimens of the Kittiwake, probably the young birds, are described as having the auriculars tipped with black.

These birds chiefly haunt the rocky promontories and islets on the British coasts, always preferring mural precipices: they are likewise widely dispersed over the world, particularly in the north, and are met with from Newfoundland to Kamtschatka, as well as in all the intermediate parts, and as far north as navigators have visited. Capt. Sabine says they are very rarely seen in the Polar Sea.

This specimen was shot on one of the Farn Islands in July, 1802.

1 *We agree with late writers in preferring the term tridactylus to the usual specific name of Rissa, being the original name given by Linnæus in the Fauna Suecica, and marking the character which distinguishes it from the rest of the genus. [Bewick's note.]*

THE SKUA GULL

(Lestris Cataractes, Temm.—*Le Goéland brun,* Buff.*)*

This stout bird is two feet in length, and between four and five from tip to tip of the extended wings, and weighs about three pounds. The bill is dark, more than two inches long, strong, much hooked, and sharp at the tip, and covered to the nostrils with a kind of cere, something like that of the Hawk tribe. The whole upper plumage is of a deep brown, edged with a dull rust colour: the under parts are of the same colours, but lighter; and in some birds, the head and throat are dashed or mixed with ash grey, and have the secondary quills tipped with white: the tail is white at the root, the shafts are of the same colour, and the webs of deep brown: the legs and toes are covered with coarse black scales; the claws are strong and hooked, the inner one more so than the rest.

This species is met with in the high latitudes of both hemispheres, where they are much more common than in the warm or temperate parts of the globe. In Capt. Cook's voyages, they are often mentioned; and, from being numerous about the Falkland Isles, the seamen called them Port-Egmont Hens. They are also common in Norway, Iceland, the Faroe, and Shetland Isles, &c. They prey not only upon fish, but also upon the lesser sorts of water-fowl, and, it is said, even upon young lambs: this, however, is doubted, and even denied: on the contrary, these birds are said to afford protection to the flocks, by driving away the Eagle, Raven, &c. which they furiously attack whenever they come within their reach. They are uncommonly courageous in defence of their own young, and seize, with the utmost vengeance, upon any animal, whether man or beast, that offers to disturb their nests; they sometimes attack the shepherds even while watching their flocks, who are obliged to guard their heads, and to ward off the blows of the assailants by holding a pointed stick towards them, against which they sometimes dash with such force as to be killed on the spot.

THE FULMAR
Mallemoke

(Procellaria glacialis, Linn.—Le Fulmar, ou Petrel Puffin gris blanc, Buff.)

Measures seventeen inches in length, and weighs about twenty-two ounces. The bill is strongly formed, and about two inches long; the hook or nail of the upper mandible, and the truncated termination or tip of the under one, are yellow; the other parts of it are greyish, and, in some specimens, blushed with red: the nostrils are contained in one sheath, divided into two tubes. The head, neck, all the under parts, and the tail, are white: back and wing coverts blue grey: quills dusky blue: legs yellowish, inclining more or less, in some specimens, to red. The body is thickly clothed with feathers upon a close fine down.

This species is peculiar to the colder climates: it has been met with in every part of both the Arctic and Antarctic regions, in all parts which navigators have been able to visit, even to the foot of those impenetrable barriers, the floating islands and eternal mountains of ice and snow.

In the northern parts of the world, the natives easily catch these heedless birds in great numbers. Pennant, speaking of those which breed on, or inhabit, the Isle of St Kilda, says: 'No bird is of such use to the islanders as this: the Fulmar supplies them with oil for their lamps, down for their beds, a delicacy for their tables; a balm for their wounds, and a medicine for their distempers.' He says also, that it is a 'certain prognosticator of the change of the wind: if it comes to land, no west wind is expected for some time; and the contrary when it returns and keeps the sea.'

These birds are extremely greedy and will devour any floating putrid substances, such as the filth from the ships, which they fearlessly follow. They also pursue the whales, but particularly the bloody track of those which are wounded, and in such great flocks as thereby sometimes to discover the prize to the fishers, with whom they generally share; for when the huge animal is no longer able to sink, the Fulmars, in multitudes, alight upon it, and ravenously pluck off and devour lumps of the blubber, till they can hold no more.

THE SHEARWATER

Skrabe, Manks Petrel, Manks Puffin, or Lyre

(Procellaria Puffinus, Linn.—Le Puffin, Buff.)

This species measures in length fifteen inches, and in breadth thirty-one, and weighs about seventeen ounces. The bill is about an inch and three quarters long; the tip black, the other parts yellowish: the tubular nostrils are not so prominent as in others of this genus. The inner coverts of the wings, and under parts of the body are white: the head, tail, thighs, and upper parts black, tinted more or less with grey: the legs are flattened on the sides, and weak; light coloured, or whitish on the fore parts, and dusky behind.

The Shearwater is found in greater or smaller numbers in almost every part of the watery world, in both hemispheres, and in every climate; but they are met with in greater abundance in the north. In the Hebrides, and other islands with which the seas of Scotland are dotted, they are caught by the natives in great numbers, and used for the same purposes as the Fulmar. Willoughby, whose excellent ornithology has thrown so much light on this branch of natural history, and cleared the paths for subsequent writers, gives the following account of the coming of these birds to breed in the Isle of Man:—

At the south end of the Isle of Man lies a little islet, divided from Man by a narrow channel, called the Calf of Man, on which are no habitations but only a cottage or two lately built. This islet is full of rabbits, which the Puffins, coming yearly, dislodge, and build in their burrows. They lay each but one egg before they sit, like the Razor-bill and Guillem, although it be the common persuasion that they lay two at a time, of which the one is always addle. The old ones early in the morning, at break of day, leave their nests and young, and the island itself, and spend the whole day in fishing at sea, never returning or once setting foot on the island before evening twilight: so that all the day the island is so quiet and still from all noise as if there were not a bird about it.

THE STORMY PETREL

Storm Finch, Little Petrel, or Mother Carey's Chicken

(Procellaria pelagica, Linn.—L' Oiseau de Tempète, Buff.)

Is the least of all the web-footed birds, measuring only about six inches in length, and thirteen in breadth. The bill is half an inch long, hooked at the tip; the nostrils tubular. The upper parts of the plumage are black, sleek, and glossed with bluish reflections: the brow, cheeks, and under parts, sooty brown: the rump, and some feathers on the sides of the tail, white: legs slender, black, and scarcely an inch and three quarters in length, from the knee joint to the end of the toes.

This bird resembles the Chimney Swallow in general appearance and the swiftness of its flight. It is met with by navigators on every part of the ocean, diving, running on foot, or skimming over the surface of the heavy rolling waves of the most tempestuous sea, quite at ease; and yet it seems to foresee the coming storm, long before the seamen can discover any appearance of its approach and make it known by flocking together under the wake of the ship, as if to shelter themselves from it, or to warn the mariners, and prepare them to guard against the danger. They are silent during the day, and their clamorous piercing cry is heard only in the night. In the breeding season they betake themselves to the promontories, where, in the fissures of the rocks, they breed and conduct their young to the watery element as soon as they are able to crawl, and immediately lead them forward to roam over the trackless ocean.

Although it has been generally said that these birds are never seen but at sea, except during the period of incubation, many instances have occurred of their having been shot inland. Latham speaks of one which was shot at Sandwich, in Kent, in a storm of wind, among a flock of Hoopoes, in January – of another shot at Walthamstow, in Essex – and of a third which was killed near Oxford. The late M. Tunstall, Esq. of Wycliffe, had one sent to him, which was shot near Bakewell, in Derbyshire; the specimen from which the above figure and description were taken, was found dead in a field near Ripon, in Yorkshire, and obligingly sent to the author by Lieut.-Col. Dalton, late of the 4th Dragoons.

THE GOOSANDER

(Mergus Merganser, Lin.*—Le Harle,* Buff.*)*

The male generally weighs about four pounds, and measures in length two feet three inches, and in breadth three feet two inches. The bill is slender, and turned a little upwards; it is three inches long from the hooked nail or tip to the corners of the mouth, but little more than two inches on the ridge; both mandibles are black on the upper and under parts, and crimson on the sides; they are sharply toothed on the edges, and on the inside of the upper, which is narrow, thin, and hard at the tip, there is a double row of smaller teeth: the tongue is furnished with a similar kind of double row, running along the middle, and edged with a kind of hairy border: the irides are commonly of a fine red colour, but in some dusky. The head is covered or crowned with a great quantity of feathers, which, when erected, form a crest; at other times they are laid flatly down, and fail over the nape of the neck: these feathers are of a glossy bottle green; the cheeks, throat, and upper fore part of the neck are dull black; the lower part of the neck, the breast, belly, vent, and inner coverts of the wings, of a beautiful cream colour: the upper part of the back, and adjoining scapulars are fine glossy black; the others bordering on the wing, white: the coverts at the setting on of the wing, black; the rest pure white: the secondary quills the same, narrowly edged with black; primaries dusky: the middle of the back and rump are ash colour; from the thighs to the sides of the tail, waved and freckled with ash and white: the tail consists of eighteen dark bluish grey feathers: the legs and feet are deep scarlet, like sealing-wax.

The Goosander is an inhabitant of cold northern latitudes, and seldom makes its appearance in the temperate or more southern climates, to which it is driven only by the inclemency of the weather, in severe winters, in search of rivers or lakes which are not bound up by the frost. It leaves this country early in the spring, and goes northward to breed, and is never seen during the summer months in any part of England; but in hard winters they are common on the freshwater pools, rivers, and fens in the East Riding of Yorkshire, and on the fens of Lincolnshire.

THE RED-BREASTED MERGANSER

(Mergus Serrator, Linn.—Le Harle huppé, Buff.)

This bird measures one foot nine inches in length, and two feet seven in breadth, and weighs about two pounds. The bill, from the tip to the angles of the mouth, is three inches in length, slender, and of a rather roundish form, hooked at the tip, and toothed on the edges: the upper mandible is dark brown, tinged with green, and edged with red; the lower one wholly red; the irides are deep red: the head, long pendent crest, and upper part of the neck, are of a glossy violet black, changing in different lights to a beautiful gilded green: the rest of the neck and belly white: the breast rusty red, spotted with black on the front, and bordered on each side with five or six white feathers, edged with black: the upper part of the back, glossy black; the lower, the rump, and sides, are prettily marked with transverse zigzag lines of brown and pale grey: the ridge of the wings, and adjoining coverts are dusky; the feathers nearest to the wings are white: the greater coverts, and some of the secondary quills, black and white; the others, and the scapulars, are also partly-coloured of the same hue: the primary quills are black; some of those next to the body tipped with white, and others of them white on the upper half, and black to their points; the white spot on the wing barred in the male by two black lines. The tail is short, its colour brown: the legs and feet of a deep saffron red. These birds, both male and female, are said to differ much in their plumage. The female is described as differing from the male in having only the rudiment of a crest, and in the white spot of the wing being crossed by only one transverse bar.

The Red-breasted Merganser is not common in Britain, particularly in the southern parts of the island; but they are met with in great flocks at Newfoundland, Greenland, and Hudson's Bay, during the summer months; they are found also in various other northern parts of the world, and in the Mediterranean sea.

THE SMEW

White Nun

(Mergus albellus, Linn.—Le petit Harle huppé, ou la Piette, Buff.)

The Smew is about the size of a Wigeon: the bill is nearly two inches long, of a dusky blue, thickest at the base, and tapering into a more slender and narrow shape towards the point: it is toothed like those of the rest of this tribe: the irides are dark: on each side of the head, an oval-shaped black patch, glossed with green, is extended from the corners of the mouth over the eyes: under side of the crest black; the other parts of the head and neck white: the breast, belly, and vent are also white, excepting a curved black stroke, pointing forward from the shoulders on each side of the upper part of the breast, which, on the lower part, has also similar strokes pointing the same way: the back, the coverts on the ridge of the wings, and the primary quills are black: the secondaries and greater coverts black, tipped with white: the middle coverts and the scapulars white: the sides, under the wings

to the tail, are agreeably variegated and crossed with dark waved lines. The tail consists of sixteen dark ash coloured feathers; the middle ones about three inches and a half long, the rest gradually tapering off shorter on each side: the legs and feet are of a bluish lead colour. This species, which seldom visits this country except in very severe winters, is at once distinguished from the rest of the *Mergi* by its black and white piebald appearance, although the individuals vary from each other in the proportion and extent of those colours on their plumage.

The Red-headed Smew had long been considered by some ornithologists as a distinct species; while others have maintained that it is the female of the Smew. It is now, however, ascertained to be the immature male of that bird.

THE WILD SWAN/BEWICK'S SWAN

Elk, Hooper, or Whistling Swan

(Anas Cygnusserus, Linn.—Le Cygne sauvage, Buff.)

The Wild Swan measures five feet in length, above seven in breadth, and weighs from thirteen to sixteen pounds. The bill is four inches long from the tip to the brow, of a yellowish white from the base to the middle, and thence to the tip, black: the bare space from the bill over the eye and eyelids is yellow: the whole plumage in adult birds is of a pure white, and next to the skin, they are clothed with a thick fine down: the legs are black.

This species generally keeps together in small flocks, or families, except in the pairing season, and at the setting in of winter. At the latter period they assemble in multitudes, particularly on the large rivers and lakes of the thinly inhabited northern parts of Europe, Asia, and America: but when the extremity of the weather threatens to become insupportable, in order to shun the gathering storm, they shape their course, high in air, in divided and diminished numbers, in search of milder climates. In such seasons they are most commonly seen in various parts of the British isles, and in other more southern countries of Europe. The same is observed of them in the North American states. They do not, however, remain longer than till the approach of spring, when they again retire northward to breed. A few, indeed, drop short, and perform that office by the way, for they are known to breed in some of the Hebrides, the Orkney, Shetland, and other solitary isles; but these are hardly worth notice: the great bodies are met with in the large rivers and lakes of Kamtschatka, North America, Iceland and Lapland. They are said to return to Iceland in flocks of about a hundred, in the spring, and also to pour in upon that island from the north, in nearly the same manner, on their way southward in the autumn. The young which are bred there remain throughout the first year.

THE MUTE SWAN

The Tame Swan

(Anas Olor, Linn.—*Le Cygne*, Buff.*)*

The plumage of this species is of the same snowy whiteness as that of the Wild Swan, and the bird is covered next the body with the same kind of fine close down; but it greatly exceeds the Wild Swan in size, weighing about twenty-five pounds, and measuring more in the length of the body and extent of the wings. This also differs in being furnished with a projecting, callous, black tubercle, or knob on the base of the upper mandible, and in the colour of the bill, which is red, with black edges and tip: the naked skin between the bill and the eyes is also of the latter colour: in the Wild Swan this bare space is yellow. There is nothing peculiar in the structure of the windpipe, which enters the lungs in a straight line.

The manners and habits are much the same in both kinds, particularly when they are in a wild state; for indeed this species cannot properly be called domesticated; they are only as it were partly reclaimed from a state of nature, and invited by the friendly and protecting hand of man to decorate and embellish the artificial lakes and pools which beautify his pleasure grounds. On these the Swan cannot be accounted a captive, for he enjoys all the sweets of liberty. Placed there, as he is the largest of all the British birds, so is he to the eye the most pleasing and elegant. What in nature can be more beautiful than the grassy-margined lake, hung round with the varied foliage of the grove, when contrasted with the pure resplendent whiteness of the majestic Swan, wafted along with erected plumes, by the gentle breeze, or floating,

189

reflected on the glossy surface of the water, while he throws himself into numberless graceful attitudes, as if desirous of attracting the admiration of the spectator!

The Swan, although possessed of the power to rule, yet molests none of the other water birds, and is singularly social and attentive to those of his own family, which he protects from every insult. While they are employed with the cares of the young brood, it is not safe to approach near them, for they will fly upon any stranger, whom they often beat to the ground by repeated blows; and they have been known by a stroke of the wing to break a man's leg. But, however powerful they are with their wings, yet a slight blow on the head will kill them.

The Swan, for ages past, has been protected on the river Thames as royal property; and it continues at this day to be accounted felony to steal their eggs. 'By this means their increase is secured, and they prove a delightful ornament to that noble river.' Latham says, 'In the reign of Edward IV, the estimation they were held in was such, that no one who possessed a freehold of less than the clear yearly value of five marks, was permitted even to keep any.' In those times, hardly a piece of water was left unoccupied by these birds, as well on account of the gratification they gave to the eye of their lordly owners, as that which they also afforded when they graced the sumptuous board at the splendid feasts of that period: but the fashion of those days is passed away, and Swans are not nearly so common now as they were formerly, being by most people accounted a coarse kind of

food, and consequently held in little estimation: but the Cygnets (so the young Swans are called) are still fattened for the table, and are sold very high, commonly for a guinea each, and sometimes for more: hence it may be presumed they are better food than is generally imagined.

This species is said to be found in great numbers in Russia and Siberia, as well as further southward, in a wild state. They are, without an owner, common on the river Trent, and on the salt-water inlet of the sea, near Abbotsbury, in Dorsetshire: they are also met with on other rivers and lakes in different parts of the British isles.

It is the generally received opinion that the Swan lives to a very great age, some say a century, and others have protracted their lives to three hundred years! Strange as this may appear, there are those who credit it: the author, however, does not scruple to hazard an opinion, that this over-stretched longevity originates only in traditionary tales, or in idle unfounded hearsay stories; as no one has yet been able to say, with certainty, to what age they attain.

The female makes her nest, concealed among the rough herbage, near the water's edge: she lays from six to eight large white eggs, and sits on them about six weeks (some say eight weeks) before they are hatched. The young do not acquire their full plumage till the second year.

It is found by experience that the Swan will not thrive if kept out of the water: confined in a courtyard, he makes an awkward figure, and soon becomes dirty, tawdry, dull, and spiritless.

THE SWAN GOOSE

Chinese, Spanish, Guinea, or Cape Goose

(Anas Cygnoides, Linn. —*L'Oie de Guinée*, Buff)

Is more than three feet in length, and of a size between the Swan and the Common Goose: it is distinguished from others of the Goose tribe by its upright and stately deportment, by having a large knob on the base of the upper mandible, and a skin, almost bare of feathers, hanging down like a pouch, or a wattle, under the throat: a white line or fillet is extended from the corners of the mouth over the front of the brow: the base of the bill is orange: irides reddish brown: a dark brown or black stripe runs down the hinder part of the neck, from the head to the back: the fore part of the neck, and the breast, are yellowish brown: the back, and all the upper parts, brownish grey, edged with a lighter colour: the sides, and the feathers which cover the thighs, are clouded nearly of the same colours as the back, and edged with white: belly white: legs orange.

It is said that these birds originally were found in Guinea only: now they are become pretty common, in a wild as well as a domesticated state, both in warm and in cold climates.

Tame Geese of this species, like other kinds, vary much, both in the colour of the bill, legs, and plumage, as well as in size; but they all retain the knob on the base of the upper mandible, and rarely want the pouch or wattle under the gullet. They are kept by the curious in various parts of England, and are more noisy than the Common Goose: nothing can stir, in the night or day, without their sounding the alarm, by their hoarse cacklings and shrill cries. They breed with the Common Goose, and their offspring are as prolific as those of any other kind. The female is smaller than the male: 'the head, neck, and breast are fulvous; paler on the upper part: the back, wings, and tail, dull brown, with pale edges: belly white: in other respects they are like the male, but the knob over the bill is smaller.'

THE CRAVAT GOOSE

Canada Goose

(Anas Canadensis, Linn.*—L'Oie à Cravate,* Buff.*)*

This is less than the Swan Goose, but taller and longer than the Tame Goose. Average weight about nine pounds; length about three feet six inches; bill dark, and two inches and a half long: irides hazel: head and neck black, with a crescent-shaped white band on the throat, which tapers off to a point on each side below the cheeks, to the hinder part of the head: the whiteness of this cravat is heightened by its contrast with the dark surrounding plumage; this mark also distinguishes it from others of the Goose tribe. All the upper parts of the plumage, the breast, and a portion of the belly, are of a dull brown, sometimes mixed with grey, and each feather is margined with a lighter colour: the lower part of the neck, the belly, vent, and upper and under tail coverts, pure white: quills and tail black: legs dingy blue.

This is another useful species which has been reclaimed from a state of nature, and domesticated and multiplied in many parts of Europe, particularly in France and Germany; but is rather uncommon in England. It is as familiar, breeds as freely, and is in every respect as valuable as the Common Goose: it is also accounted a great ornament on ponds near gentlemen's seats. Buffon says, 'Within these few years, many hundreds inhabited the great canal at Versailles, where they lived familiarly with the Swans: they were oftener on the grassy margins than in the water. There is at present a great number of them on the magnificent pools that decorate the charming gardens of Chantilly.'

The wild stock whence these birds were taken are found in the northern parts of America; they are one of those immense families, which, when associated with others of the same genus, are said, at certain seasons, to darken the air like a cloud, and to spread themselves over the lakes and swamps in innumerable multitudes.

THE BRENT GOOSE

(Anas Bernicla, Linn.—*Le Cravant*, Buff.*)*

This is of nearly the same shape and size as the Bernacle, from which it differs in the colour of its plumage, being mostly of a uniform brown, the feathers edged with ash: the upper parts, breast and neck, are darker than the belly, which is more mixed and dappled with paler cinereous and grey: the bead and upper half of the neck are black, excepting a white patch on each side of the latter, near the throat: the lower part of the back and rump are also black: the tail coverts above and below, and the vent, white: tail, quills, and legs dusky: the hill is dark, rather of a narrow shape, and only about an inch and a half long: the irides are light hazel. In the females and the younger birds, the plumage is not so distinctly marked, and the white spots on the sides of the neck are often mixed with dusky.

The Brent Geese, like other species of the same genus, quit the rigours of the north in winter, and spread themselves southward in greater or less numbers, impelled forward, according to the severity of the season, in search of milder climates. They are then met with on the British shores, and spend the winter months in the rivers, lakes, and marshes in the interior parts, feeding mostly upon the roots, and also on the blades of the long coarse grasses and plants which grow in the water: but indeed their varied modes of living, as well as their other habits and propensities, and their migrations, haltings, breeding places, &c. do not differ materially from those of the other numerous families of the Wild Geese. Buffon gives a detail of the devastations which they made, in the hard winters of 1740 and 1765, upon the corn fields, on the coasts of Picardy, in France, where they appeared in such immense flocks, that the people were literally raised (*en masse* we suppose) in order to attempt their extirpation, which, however, it seems they could not effect, and a change in the weather only, caused these unwelcome visitants to depart.

THE EIDER DUCK

St Cuthbert's Duck

(Anas mollissima, Linn.—*L'Eider,* Buff.*)*

This wild, but valuable, species is of a size between the Goose and the Domestic Duck. The full-grown old males measure about two feet two inches in length, and two feet eighteen in breadth, and weigh from six to above seven pounds. The head is large; the middle of the neck small, with the lower part of it very broad, so as to form a hollow between the shoulders, which, while the bird is sitting at ease, seems as if fitted to receive its reclining head. The bill is of a dirty yellowish horn colour, dark in the middle, and measures two inches and a half: the upper mandible is forked towards each eye, and is covered with white feathers on the sides. The upper part of the head is of a soft velvet black, divided behind by a dull white stroke pointing downwards: the feathers from the nape of the neck to the throat, are long, or puffed out, overhanging the upper part of the neck, and look as if they had been clipped off at the lower ends: they have the appearance of a pale pea-green velvet shag, with a white line dropping downward from the auriculars on each side. The cheeks, chin, upper part of the neck, back, and lesser wing coverts, are white: the scapulars, and secondary quills, next the body, dirty white: bastard wings, and primary quills brown; secondaries and greater coverts the same, but much darker: the lower broad part of the neck, on the front, to the breast, is of a buff colour: the breast, belly, vent, rump, and tail coverts are of a deep black: tail feathers hoary brown: legs short, and yellow: webs and nails dusky. The female is nearly of the same shape, though less than the male; but her plumage is quite different, the ground colour being of a reddish brown, prettily crossed with waved black lines; and in some specimens the neck, breast, and belly, are tinged with ash: the wings are crossed with two bars of white: quills dark: the neck is marked with longitudinal dusky streaks, and the belly is deep brown, spotted obscurely with black.

THE MUSK DUCK

Cairo, Guinea, or Indian Duck

(Anas moschata, Linn.—*Le Canard Musque,* Buff.)

This species is much larger than the Common Duck, measuring about two feet in length. The irides are pale yellow; the bill, from the tip to the protuberance on the brow, is more than two inches long. Domestication has made a great variation in the plumage of these birds, but they are all alike in having a fleshy knob on the base of the bill, and a naked, red, warty skin extending from that and the chin to above the eyes, and in having the crown of the head rather tufted and black, which they can erect at pleasure. The bill red, except about the nostrils and tip, where it is brown; the cheeks, throat, and fore part of the neck, white, irregularly marked with black: the belly, from the breast to the thighs, white. The general colour of the rest of the plumage is deep brown, darkest and glossed with green, on the back, rump, quills, and tail; the two outside feathers of the latter, and the first three of the quills, are white. The legs are short and thick, and as well as the toes, vary from red to yellow.

Ornithologists are in doubt as to the country to which these birds originally belonged; it is, however, agreed, that they are natives of the warm climates. Pennant says they are met with, wild, about the lake Baikal, in Asia; Ray, that they are natives of Louisiana; Maregrave, that they are met with in Brazil; and Buffon, that they are found in the overflowed savannas of Guiana, where they feed in the daytime upon the wild rice, and return in the evening to the sea; he adds, 'they nestle on the trunks of rotten trees; and after the young are hatched, the mother takes them one after another by the bill and throws them into the water.'

These birds have obtained the name of Musk Duck from their musky smell, which arises from the liquor secreted in the glands on the rump. They breed readily with the Common Duck, forming an intermediate kind, better suited to the table than either of the parents. The Hybrids do not appear to be productive.

THE MALLARD
Common Wild Duck
(Anas Boschas, Linn.—*Le Canard Sauvage*, Buff.*)*

Weighs from thirty-six to forty ounces, and measures twenty-three inches in length, and thirty-five in breadth. The bill is of a yellowish green colour, not very flat, about an inch broad, and two and a half long: the head and upper half of the neck are of a glossy deep changeable green, terminated in the middle of the neck by a white collar: the lower part of the neck, the breast, and shoulders, are of a deep vinous chesnut: the covering scapular feathers are of a kind of silvery white; those underneath rufous; and both are prettily crossed with small waved threads of brown: wing coverts ash: quills brown; and between these intervenes the beauty-spot which crosses the closed wing in a transverse oblique direction: it is of a rich glossy purple, with violet or green reflections, and bordered by a double streak of black and white. The belly is of a pale grey, delicately pencilled with numberless narrow waved dusky lines, which, on the sides and long feathers that reach over the thighs, are more strongly and distinctly marked: the upper and under tail coverts, lower part of the back, and the rump, are black: the latter glossed with green: the four middle tail feathers are also black, with purple reflections, and, like those of the Domestic Drake, are stiffly curled upwards; the rest are sharp-pointed, and fade off to the exterior sides, from a brown to a dull white: legs, toes, and webs red.

The plumage of the female is very different from that of the male, and partakes of none of his beauties except the spot on the wings. All the other parts are plain brown, marked with black. She lays from ten to sixteen greenish white eggs, and rears her young, generally in the most sequestered mosses or bogs, far from the haunts of man, and hidden from his sight among reeds and rushes. To her young helpless unfledged family (and they are nearly three months before they can fly) she is a fond, attentive, and watchful parent.

THE SCAUP DUCK

(Anas Marila, Linn.)

Some of this species, it is said, weigh only a pound and a half, while others exceed that weight by eight or nine ounces, and measure, when stretched out, nearly twenty inches in length, and thirty-two in breadth. The bill is broad and flat, more than two inches long, and of a fine pale blue or lead colour, with the nail black: irides bright deep yellow: the head and upper half of the neck are black, glossed with green: the lower part of the latter, and the breast, are of a sleek plain black: the throat, rump, upper and under coverts of the tail, and part of the thighs, are of the same colour, but dull, and more inclining to brown. The tail, when spread out, is fan-shaped, and consists of fourteen short brown feathers: the hack, scapulars, wing coverts, and tertials, are varied from white to deeper shades of pale ash, and ash brown, and are prettily marked with delicately freckled, or more distinctly pencilled transverse dark waved lines: the bastard wings, greater coverts, and the exterior webs of the first two or three primary quills, and the tips of all the rest, are deep brown, sprinkled with white, and crossed with narrow waved white lines: some of the primary quills towards the body, are white; the bases of the secondaries, of the same colour, form an oblique bar across the wings, which is stopped by a single under tertial feather, of plain brown, with green reflections: the belly is white, and shaded off towards the vent with the same kind of sprinkled and waved lines. The legs are short; toes long, and, as well as the outer or lateral webs of the inner toes, are of a dirty pale blue colour; all the joints and the rest of the webs are dusky. The Scaup Duck quits the rigours of the dreary north in the winter months, and in that season only is met with, in small numbers, on various parts of the British shores.

The female differs so much from the male, as to have been considered a distinct species, and figured as such in the *British Miscellany*. (Montagu.)

THE SHOVELER

Blue-wing Shoveler, Kertlutock, or Broad-bill

(Anas clypeata, Linn.—Le Souchet, Buff.)

The Shoveler is less than the Wild Duck, weighing about twenty-two ounces, and measuring twenty-one inches in length. The bill is black, three inches long, very broad or spread out, and rounded like a spoon at the end, with the nail hooked inward and small: the insides of the mandibles are remarkably well furnished with thin pectinated rows, which fit into each and through which no dirt can pass, while the bird is sifting the small worms and insects from amongst the mud, by the edges of the water, where it is continually searching for them: the irides are of a fine pure yellow; the head and upper half of the neck of a dark glossy changeable green: the lower part of the neck, the breast, and scapulars, white: the back is brown: belly and sides chesnut bay, and the wing coverts of a fine pale sky blue, terminated with white tips, which form an oblique stripe across the wings, and an upper border to the beauty spot, or spangle, which is of a glossy changeable bronze, or resplendent green,

and also divides or crosses the wings in the same direction: the greater quills and the tail are dusky, but in the latter the outside feathers, and the edges of some of the adjoining ones, are white: a ring of white also encircles the rump and the vent, behind which the feathers under the tail are black: legs and feet red. The female is smaller than the male, from which she also differs greatly in the colours of her plumage, the coverts and spangle spot on her wings being less brilliant, and the other parts composed of white, grey, and rusty, crossed with curved dusky lines, giving her much the appearance of the Common Wild Duck. She makes her nest, lined with withered grasses, on the ground, in the midst of the largest tufts of rushes or coarse herbage, in the most inaccessible part of the slaky marsh: she lays ten or twelve pale rusty-coloured eggs; and as soon as the young are hatched, they are conducted to the water by the parent birds, who watch and guard them with the greatest care.

THE PINTAIL DUCK

Sea Pheasant, Cracker, or Winter Duck

(Anas acuta, Linn.*—Le Canard à longue queue,* Buff.*)*

This handsome-looking bird is twenty-eight inches in length, and thirty-eight in breadth, and weighs about twenty-four ounces. The bill is rather long, black in the middle, and blue on the edges: the irides reddish: the head and throat are of a rusty brown, mottled with small dark spots, and tinged behind the ears with purple: the nape and upper part of the neck are dusky, margined by a narrow white line, which runs down on each side, and falling into a broader stripe of the same colour, extends itself on the fore part as far as the breast; the rest of the neck, the breast, and the upper part of the back, are elegantly pencilled with black and white waved lines: the lower back and sides of the body are undulated in the same manner, but with lines more freckled and paler: the scapulars are long and pointed, each feather black down the middle, with white edges: the coverts of the wings are ash brown, tipped dull orange: below these the wing is obliquely crossed by the beauty spot of glossy bronze purple green, with a lower border of black and white: this spangle is formed by the outer webs and tips of the middle quills: the rest of the quills are dusky. All the tail feathers are of a brown ash colour, with pale edges, except the two middle ones, which are black, glossed with green, longer than the others, and end in a point: the belly and the sides of the vent are white: under tail coverts black: legs and feet small, and of a lead colour. The female is less than the male, and her plumage is plainer, all the upper parts being brown, with each feather margined with white, inclining to red or yellow: the greater covert, and secondary quills are tipped with cream colour and white. The fore part of the neck, the breast, and the belly, to the vent, are of a dull white, spotted with brown. The tail is long and pointed, but the two middle feathers do not extend beyond the rest. These birds do not visit temperate and warm climates in great numbers, except in very severe winters.

199

THE TUFTED DUCK[1]

(Anas fuligula, Linn.—Le petit Morillon, Brisson.)

This is a plump, round, and short-shaped species. The male is distinguished by a pendent crest, overhanging the nape of the neck, two inches in length. The weight is about two pounds, length eighteen inches. The bill is broad, of a dark lead colour; the nail black: irides deep orange: the head is black, glossed with purple: the neck, breast, and all the upper parts, are of a deep brown or black: the scapulars faintly powdered or sprinkled with light spots, so minute as not to be observed at a short distance. The wings are crossed by a narrow white bar: the belly, sides, and under coverts of the wings, are of a pure white: the vent white, mixed with dusky. The tail consists of fourteen very short feathers: the legs are of a dark lead colour; webs black. The female is of a browner colour than the male, and has no crest.

The habits, manners, and haunts of this species are much the same as those of the Golden-eye, and they return northward about the same time. Latham says 'the French allow these birds to be eaten on maigre days and in lent; as they do also the Scoter: but though the flesh of the latter is now and then tolerable, that of the Tufted Duck is seldom otherwise than excellent.'

1 *The tuft is sometimes wanting, and in that state has been made a distinct species. Montagu. [Bewick's note.]*

THE CORMORANT

Great Black Cormorant

(Pelecanus Carbo, Linn.—*Le Cormoran,* Buff.*)*

The weight of this species varies from four to seven pounds, and the size from thirty-two inches to three feet four or five in length, and from four feet to four feet six inches in breadth. The bill measures four inches: it is of a dark horn colour, and the tip or nail of the upper mandible is much hooked and sharp: the lower bill is compressed, and covered about the gape with a naked yellowish skin, extended under the chin and throat, where it hangs loose, and forms a kind of pouch, which, together with the springing blades on each side, forming its rim, is capable of distention that enables the bird to swallow prey apparently too large to be admitted into its throat: the eyes, which have a remarkably wild stare, look like two little greenish glass globes. The crown of the head, and the neck, are black: on the hinder part of the former the feathers are elongated, and form a loose short crest. In some specimens the throat is white, with a kind of stripe passing from it upwards behind each eye; in others the cheeks and throat are mixed with brown and white; and again, in others the head and neck are streaked with scratches of the latter colour: the middle of the belly is white, with a patch of the same colour over each thigh: all the under parts, however, together with the back and rump, are glossy blue black, with green reflections: the shoulders, scapulars, and wing coverts are of a bronze brown, tinged and glossed with green, and each feather is bordered with bluish black: the secondary quills are nearly of the same colour: the coverts and the primaries are dusky. The tail consists of fourteen stiff dark feathers: the legs are thick, strong, black, and coarse. At sea, or on the inland lakes, they make a terrible havoc. From the greatest height they drop down upon the object of pursuit, dive after it with the rapidity of a dart, and seize the victim; then emerging, with the fish across the bill, with a kind of twirl, throw it up into the air, and catching it head foremost, swallow it whole.

THE SHAG

Skart, Scarfe, or Green Cormorant

(Pelecanus graculus, Linn.—*Le petit Cormoran, ou le Nigaud,* Buff.*)*

The aspect altogether, the character, habits, and the places of abode of this species are nearly like those of the Cormorant; but they do not associate, and these make their nests on the rugged crevices of the rocky precipices or projecting cliffs which overhang the sea, while the others make theirs on the summits above them; and these are at once distinguished from the others by the greenness of the upper, and brownness of the under plumage, and also in being of a much less size; the largest Shags weighing only about four pounds, and measuring nearly two feet six inches in length, and three feet eight in breadth. The bill is of a more slender make, but nearly as long as that of the Cormorant; the head, in the male, is crested in the same manner and its tail, consisting of twelve stiff feathers stained with green, is also of the same form, and hoary or dirty appearance, as that of the Cormorant: the crown of the head, hinder part of the neck, lower back, and rump, are of a plain black, or very dark green, shining like satin: the upper back, or shoulders, together with the scapulars and wings, are nearly of the same colour, but with a tinge of bronze brown, and each feather is distinctly edged with purple glossed black: the under parts are clouded with dusky dirty white and brown.

The Shag is as voracious as the Cormorant, and like that bird, after having over-gorged, is often found on shore in a stupefied state. In swimming they carry their head very erect, while the body seems nearly submerged, and from their feathers not being quite impervious to the water, they do not remain very long upon it at a time, but are frequently seen flying about, or sitting on the rocks, flapping the moisture from their wings, or keeping them for some time expanded, to dry in the sun and the wind. Notwithstanding the strong and offensive smell emitted from the Shags and the Cormorants, some instances are not wanting of their having been eaten in this country.

THE GANNET
Gan, Soland, or Solan Goose
(Pelecanus bassanus, Linn.—*Le Fou de Bassan,* Buff.*)*

The Gannet is generally about seven pounds in weight, three feet in length, and six in breadth. The bill is of a pale or lead-coloured blue, six inches long, a little jagged on the edges, strong and straight to the tip, which is inclined a little downwards: the upper bill is furnished with a distinct rib or ridge, running along from the tip nearly to its base, on each side of which it is furrowed, without any visible appearance of nostrils: the tongue is small, and placed far within the mouth, all the inside of which is black: a darkish line passes from the brow over the eyes, which are surrounded with a naked blue skin, and, like those of the Owl, are set in the head so as to look nearly straight forward, and the extreme paleness of the irides gives them a keen wild stare. The gape of the mouth is very wide, and seems more lengthened, by a slip of naked black skin, which is extended on each side from the corners beyond the cheeks: these features of its countenance, altogether, give

it somewhat the appearance of wearing spectacles. A loose black bare dilatable skin, capable of great distension, hung from the blades of the under bill, and extended over the throat, serves it as a pouch to carry provisions to its mate, or its young. The body is flat and well clothed with feathers; the neck long: the crown of the head, nape, and, in some specimens, the hinder part of the neck, are of a buff colour; greater quills and bastard wings black, and the rest of the plumage white. The tail is wedge-shaped, and consists of twelve tapering sharp-pointed feathers. The legs and feet are nearly of the same colour and conformation as those of the Cormorant, but are curiously marked by three pea-green stripes, which run down each leg, and branch off along the toes. The male and female are nearly alike, but the young birds, during the first year, appear as if they were of a distinct species, for their plumage is then of a dusky colour, speckled all over with triangular white spots.

THE GREAT AUK

Northern Penguin, or Gair-fowl

(Alca impennis, Linn.—Le Grand Pingouin, Buff.)

The length of this bird, to the end of the toes, is three feet. The bill is black, and four inches and a quarter long; both mandibles are crossed obliquely with several ridges and furrows, which meet at the edges. Two oval-shaped white spots occupy nearly the whole space between the bill and the eyes: the head, back part of the neck, and all the upper parts of the body and wings are covered with short, soft, glossy black feathers, excepting a white stroke across the wings, formed by the tips of the lesser quills: the whole under side of the body is white: the wings are very short, not exceeding four inches and a quarter from the tips of the longest quill feathers to the first joint: legs black, short, and placed near the vent.

From the difficulty with which these birds fly or walk, they are seldom seen out of the water, and it is remarked by seamen, that they never wander beyond soundings. The female is said to lay only one egg, which she deposits and hatches on a ledge close to the sea-mark: it is of a very large size, being about six inches in length, of a white colour, streaked with lines of a purple cast, and blotched with dark rusty spots at the thicker end.

This species is not numerous anywhere: it inhabits Norway, Iceland, the Faroe Isles, Greenland, and other cold regions of the north, but is seldom seen on the British shores.

The Gair-fowl described by Martin, in his voyage to St Kilda, and account of that island, published in 1698, differs in some particulars from the foregoing: he says, 'it is larger than the Solan Goose, black, red about the eyes, has a large white spot under each eye, a long broad bill; stands erect, has short wings, cannot fly; lays one egg, twice the size of that of the Solan Goose, variously speckled with black, green, and dusky spots.'

THE RAZOR-BILL

Auk, Murre, Falk, Marrot, or Scout

(Alca torda, Linn.—*Le Pingouin,* Buff.*)*

The wings of this species are more furnished with feathers, and longer in proportion to the size of the bird, than those of the last; they measure, extended, about twenty-seven inches: the length of the bird, from bill to tail, is eighteen. The bill is black, strong, curved towards the point, and sharply edged; the upper mandible is crossed with four transverse grooves, and the under one with three, the broadest of which is white, and forms a band across them both: the inside of the mouth is yellow: the base of the bill is covered with feathers a great way forward, upon which, on each side, is placed a narrow, white streak, which passes to the corner of the eye; another white stripe or bar crosses each wing obliquely: the upper part of the head, hinder part of the neck, back, rump, and tail coverts are of a soft glossy black: the cheeks, chin, and throat are of a dull sooty dark brown; ridge and pinions of the wings, light brown: coverts and quills dusky: legs black.

These birds associate with the Guillemots, and also breed in the same places. About the beginning of May they take possession of the highest impending rocks, for the purpose of incubation, and upon the ledges of these rocks they congregate in great numbers, sitting closely together, tier above tier, and row above row: there they deposit their single large egg on the bare rock; and notwithstanding the numbers of them, thus mixed together, yet no confusion takes place, for each bird knows her own egg, and hatches it in that situation. It has often excited wonder that as the eggs have no nest or bedding to rest upon, they are not rolled off into the sea by gales of wind, or upon being touched by the birds. The egg of this Auk is three inches long, of a greenish white colour, irregularly marked with dark spots. They are gathered, with other kinds, in great numbers, by the neighbouring inhabitants, from the rocky promontories in various parts of the British Isles.

THE PUFFIN

Mullet, Coulterneb, Sea-parrot, Pope, or Willock

(Alca Arctica, Linn.—*Le Macareux,* Buff.*)*

The Puffin weighs about twelve ounces, and measures twelve inches in length, and twenty-one in breadth. Its singular bill looks not unlike a kind of sheath slipped over both mandibles. At the base, it is rimmed with a white border, the two corners of which project above the brow, and below the chin. It is about the same in length, curved towards the point, compressed vertically, very flat, and transversely furrowed on the sides; the half of it adjoining to the head is smooth, and of a fine lead-coloured blue; the other part, to the tip, red: the nostrils are placed in long narrow slits, near the edge of the bill: the corners of the mouth, when closed, are curiously puckered: the eyes are protected by small protuberances, both above and below: the edges of the eyelids are crimson: irides grey: the chin and cheeks are white, bordered with grey, the latter much puffed up with feathers, which makes the head look large and round. From behind each eye, the feathers are separated, forming a narrow line, which reaches to the hinder part of the head: the crown of the head, hinder part of the neck, and upper part of the plumage are black, and a collar of the same colour encircles the neck: the under parts are white: the tail consists of sixteen feathers: the legs are reddish orange.

The Puffin, though it takes wing with difficulty, can fly with rapidity. It walks with a wriggling awkward gait. In tempestuous weather it takes shelter in holes in the nearest rocks, or in those made by the rabbit on the beach, among the bent grass, in which it sits dozing till the return of calm weather. Various kinds of fish, such as small crabs, shrimps, sprats, and also seaweeds, are said to be the food upon which they live. The female makes no nest; she deposits her single whitish coloured egg upon the bare mould, in a hole dug out and formed in the ground, by her mate and herself, for that purpose; or in those that they find ready-made by the rabbits, which they easily dislodge.

THE LITTLE AUK

Little Black and White Diver

(*Alca alle*, Linn.—*Le petit Guillemot*, Buff.)

This plump round-shaped bird, measures about nine inches in length. The bill is black, short, thick, strong, and convex; it is feathered from the corners of the mouth halfway forward towards the point. The crown of the head is flat and black; all the upper parts of the plumage are of the same colour, except a narrow bar of white, formed by the tips of the lesser quills across the wings, and the scapulars, which are streaked downwards with the same:[1] the cheeks and under parts are white: legs and toes yellowish; webs dusky.

These birds are inhabitants of Spitzbergen and Greenland, and are also met with at Newfoundland, where they are called Ice Birds. Captain Sabine says, 'it is not common in the Polar sea; its great breeding station is in the northern part of Baffin's Bay.' They are rare visitants of the British Isles. That from which the above figure and description were taken, was caught alive on the Durham coast, and was, for a short time, fed with grain.

1 *Some specimens have a white spot below each eye. [Bewick's note.]*